A GIRL'S GUIDE TO BEING
GREAT

Cultivating a Generation of *Grounded, Gracious*, and *Gutsy* Girls

A GIRL'S GUIDE TO BEING
GREAT

Cultivating a Generation of *Grounded, Gracious*, and *Gutsy* Girls

BY

RHONDA G. MINCEY

ISBN 978-0-9882039-4-5

Contact us at:
Great Success, LLC.
7 Venture Drive, Suite 104-116
Bluffton, SC 29910

www.rhondamincey.com

The stories are true, but the names are changed.
The scenarios are hypothetical.

Printed in the United States of America

Thanks from the girls

"Thank you, Ms. Mincey, for writing this book for girls. It helped me so much in middle school; now, I am a junior in high school. I've passed the book down to my younger sister."

"Thank you for writing a book for girls because we need inspiration for our situations."

"Now I know I'm a beautiful, valuable, phenomenal young girl, and I am loved."

"To be a leader, you must be true to yourself."

"You should never smoke or do drugs."

"Like a diamond, I will rise and shine."

"Every choice I make has a consequence."

"I will set my values high."

"I will try to make great decisions throughout my life."

"Your speech was a big turning point in my life."

"I will believe in myself."

"Bad choices will affect my future."

"Choices can be life-changing."

"I will be careful who I allow in my life."

Thanks from parents, facilitators, and administrators

"Mrs. Rhonda, we cannot begin to thank you for all you have done for our daughter & the young women of MCR. She has made tremendous gains in confidence and presentation of herself to others.

Your program and guidance with these girls will continue tremendously impacting them in the next stages of their education and lives. We will always be grateful to you and your dedication. We wish you and your program blessings in the years ahead."
~ Ms. Dixon (Great Girl parent)

"This program can open up a girl's word."
~ Community Volunteer

"I wish I had this program when I was a girl."
~ Great Girls Club™ Facilitator

"My commitment to make the Great Girls celebration memorable originates with my desire to see these young ladies reach their greatest potential. I desire to use the Great Girls curriculum to present them with foundation cornerstones they will use to build their futures and their dreams.
~ Debby Bryan, LSW, Great Girls Club™ Facilitator

"If girls know who they are, the test scores and grades will take care of themselves."
~ Mr. Robert Candillo, Principal

Table of Contents

A GIRL'S GUIDE TO BEING GREAT

ACKNOWLEDGEMENTS

I want to thank:

My mom, Dorothy Zeigler, who told me and showed me when I was a little girl that I could conquer the world.

Douglas Mincey, my husband, friend, and "better half" who supports my every dream.

The schools who have partnered with me to develop a dynamic program for girls centered on this book:

The people who have given me their time, financial support, and resources to help girls reach their full potential over the years.

My "unofficial" mentors - whom I look up to and who have inspired me to be great and

The girls who apply the principles of this book to their lives.

INTRODUCTION

Hey, young lady.

After hosting many workshops and meet-ups for girls like you, I felt this deep urge to reach out to even more of you. Why? Because every girl, including you, deserves to know how truly amazing she is and how to unlock her full potential. So, I wrote this book hoping to inspire and uplift millions of girls everywhere.

When I chatted with girls, I often asked, "What do you think you're meant to be?" Some said they're destined to change lives, to lead, or even to surpass what everyone expects of them. And guess what? They're right. And so are you. You've got this spark inside you, this purpose, and you're meant for big things. Remember, how you see yourself shapes who you become.

Let's talk about Cindy for a second. She attended just a few of my sessions. But by the end, she sent me this sweet email about how telling herself she's beautiful every day made a world of difference. She's a "sponge" – soaking up every positive vibe and craving more. Just a straightforward message transformed her outlook and choices.

But not everyone is like Cindy. Some girls attended my sessions for months but struggled to shift their mindset. It's not always easy, but it's so worth it.

Here's the thing: Sometimes, all it takes is one chapter or sentence from this book to click. If you open your heart to the messages and lessons in this book, you're on the path to becoming grounded, gracious, and gutsy (bold). And trust me, the world needs more girls like that.

As you grow and evolve, know I'm your biggest cheerleader! So, flip that page and embrace a mindset that'll shape you into an incredible woman.

You got this!

Challenging you and cheering you on with love and support,

Mrs. Mincey 🖤

1

REALIZING YOUR POWER

"Never underestimate the power of dreams and the influence of the human spirit. We are all the same in this notion: The potential for greatness lives within each of us."
~Wilma Rudolph (1940 - 1994)
First American woman runner to win three gold medals at a single Olympics

---

I've met and talked to many girls through my line of work. Some of them have been bright, outgoing, and shined with confidence, but others have been sad, withdrawn, and unsure of themselves. Some of them have been leaders, while still others have been followers. However, what they had in common was that they were young ladies who wanted love and acceptance. Don't you? I still do.

Several years ago, I saw two girls walking in my old neighborhood. They had on tight shorts and shirts that left little to the imagination. I knew they would attract attention from boys, but I also knew it would be the wrong attention.

This realization led me to ask myself several questions: Do these girls think this is the only way to meet a boy? Do they realize that their intelligence and personality make them attractive? Do they even *know* what gifts they have inside of them? Do you? Or are you like Karla?

Karla was in middle school when I met her. She was well-spoken and had the potential to be a great leader, but she had a habit of following people who did not have her best interest at heart. She had a bad reputation with boys and would get into fights with girls. In addition, Karla used language that was not proper for a young lady. So, when she joined ROTC at her high school, I was excited for her because I believed it could help her become a strong leader and positive role model.

I felt proud of Karla when I saw her in her ROTC navy blue uniform and shiny, polished black shoes! She looked like a professional young lady instead of a troublemaker. I knew she was on the right track and rejoiced with her. Can you imagine my shock and disappointment when I heard the principal sent Karla to another school for threatening to fight a girl?

No matter how much I talked to Karla to encourage her, she did not change her ways; instead, she seemed to get worse! Her language was so foul on Facebook that I had to block her from being my "friend." I knew that Karla had family issues that probably contributed to her behavior. Still, I also believed that a big part of her problem was that she did not know a simple truth: she was born for greatness. Karla's way of thinking (about life and herself) was not positive, and it showed in her behavior.

> Still, I also believed that a big part of her problem was that she did not know a simple truth: she was a smart and powerful young lady who was born for a purpose.

Point to Ponder
Do you think Karla knew that she had greatness inside of her? Why or why not?

_____

_____

1. Remove the Limits

Karla's mindset and behavior placed unnecessary limitations on her life, such as the people she associated with and the schools she could attend. She reminded me of a caterpillar before it became a butterfly.

At first glance, a caterpillar may not be the prettiest creature one might see. As a matter of fact, when I first saw a caterpillar, I thought that it was just an unattractive, hairy worm that made my skin crawl. It was fat and short and moved slowly on the ground as though it had no purpose. Because of this, I had forgotten that the caterpillar's existence is far more than I gave it credit for. You see, a caterpillar transforms and eventually becomes a beautiful butterfly. So, instead of crawling and being limited to the ground, it flies freely from flower to flower. Instead of being "unattractive" to some, it is now a creature of vibrant beauty that delights the eye!

Maybe you feel you are not good enough or pretty enough. Think again. Look again. Just like a caterpillar, you are beautiful from the inside out. Perhaps someone placed limitations on you about what you can do, but regardless of your situation, it does not define who you are or what you can accomplish.

> Maybe you feel you are not good enough or pretty enough. Think again. Look again.
> Just like a caterpillar, you are beautiful from the inside out.

Since greatness is already in you, you don't have to try to become great. Like the caterpillar, you already have inside of you all that you need to be great; it might just take some time to develop it. So I challenge you to see yourself for who you are: beautiful, divinely designed, and someone who can reach new heights. It's time to break free from the constraints that hold you back and prevent you from reaching your full potential. Don't let fear, doubt, or societal norms limit your dreams. You can smash through those barriers and unlock doors of opportunity.

Look at Gitanjali Rao, an American inventor, author, social activist, and a science, technology, engineering, and mathematics student and advocate. She won the Discovery Education 3M Young Scientist Challenge and was recognized on Forbes 30 Under 30 for her innovations. Gitanjali developed solutions to address real-world problems like clean water and cyberbullying. She refused to let age or perceived limitations stop her from making an impact. You, too, can break down those walls, whether imposed by others or created by your self-doubt.

Point to Ponder
What did you learn about limitations?
_____

_____

2. Average Is Not an Option
There is a saying that average is "the top of the bottom and the bottom of the top." But "great" girls aren't just average. Girls in the GREAT Girls Club® are **G**enerous, **R**eal (authentic), **E**ducated, **A**mazing, and **T**alented. They strive to do their best in everything.

On the other hand, ordinary people just blend in with the crowd, limiting themselves. For example, an *average* girl may get looked over for specific opportunities because she hasn't demonstrated that she is different from her peers. They also tend to settle for less. For instance, they don't mind coming in second, third, or last place. Or, they are okay with getting a "C" in a class if they pass it. If you have this attitude, you might achieve some of your goals (if you've set *low* goals for yourself). However, this carefree attitude will most likely stop you from being the best person you can be, reaching high ideals, and excelling in life.

So let's clarify one thing: You are meant not to blend in, get by, or settle for mediocrity. Instead, your dreams, aspirations, and talents are meant to be extraordinary.

Look at Simone Biles, the phenomenal gymnast who pushed the boundaries of what was thought possible in her sport. She defied expectations and redefined what it means to be a champion. Remember, aiming for average won't set your soul on fire.

> Develop an attitude of excellence instead of an attitude of average.

Declare that you will be extraordinary instead of average. Don't just do what people ask of you; go the extra mile. Take the "me" out of the mediocre and dig deep inside of you to do and be your best!

If you are running a race, why not train to win? If you are going to school, why not do your absolute best? Develop an attitude of excellence instead of a mindset of average.

I'm not saying you should be perfect because no one is perfect. Being your best means that you should put your all in everything you do. After all, your hard work and sacrifice reward you. But laziness does not.

Point to Ponder
Is being "average" okay with you? Why or why not?

_____

_____

_____

3. You are Full of Power

Listen up because this is a truth you need to know deep in your bones: You possess boundless power. It's time to recognize the strength within you and embrace it fearlessly. Remember, you can make a difference, create, lead, and change the world around you.

> *"We cannot succeed when half of us are held back. We call upon our sisters around the world to be brave, to embrace the strength within themselves and realize their full potential."*
> ~Malala Yousafzai

Look at Malala Yousafzai, a young Pakistani activist who stood up for girls' education in the face of adversity. Despite immense challenges, she used her voice to fight for what she believed in and became the youngest Nobel Prize laureate. Malala declared, *"We cannot succeed when half of us are held back. We call upon our sisters around the world to be brave, to embrace the strength within themselves, and realize their full potential."*

Malala understood that everyone has potential. But she didn't stop there. She gave every girl a call of action to reach hers. And like her, you can achieve greatness at a young age despite your background or circumstances.

So don't sell yourself short. The world needs your gifts. You have the potential to do anything you set your mind to. And you can influence, inspire, and encourage others to accomplish their dreams. Will you tap into your power to do great things?

_____

_____

Point to Ponder
What do you have the potential to do or become?

_____

_____

Affirmation
There is more to me than I realize, so I will do my best to live up to my potential.

I AM MY OWN "SHERO"

Reflect and Write

1. What does being "more" mean to you?

_____

_____

_____

2. What three things are you "more than?" For example, "I am more than average."

_____

_____

_____

3. What three things are you made to be? You can write an adjective, such as "I am made to be <u>awesome,</u>" or a noun, such as "I am made to be <u>a leader,</u>" or a combination of both.

_____

_____

_____

4. Write an affirmation that Karla could say that might help her change her behavior.

_____

_____

_____

_____

5. Why should you always strive to do your best?

_____

_____

_____

_____

A GIRL'S GUIDE TO BEING GREAT

Bonus Scenario for Realizing Your Power

Sarah sat in her bedroom, surrounded by textbooks and notes, her dreams out of reach. She had always wanted to make a difference in the world, but it seemed impossible with her family struggling to make ends meet and her school needing more resources. Doubt whispered in her ear, telling her she wasn't capable of greatness. But little did Sarah know that a spark would ignite within her.

One day, while browsing the internet, Sarah stumbled upon a video about a young girl named Maya. Maya had grown up in a similar circumstance, facing adversity at every turn. Yet, she defied the odds and became a successful entrepreneur, empowering others. Something within Sarah shifted while watching Maya's story unfold. A newfound determination ignited in her heart, whispering that she had the power to create change.

Sarah started small, reaching out to her classmates and forming a study group to support each other. Together, they discovered they were not alone in their struggles, and their collective strength propelled them forward. Sarah realized they were powerful beyond measure when they united as a team.

Sarah started a blog to share her thoughts and experiences, embracing her love for writing. She poured her heart into each word, reaching out to others who faced similar challenges. Through her writings, she discovered the power of her voice and the impact it could have on those who needed it most.

As Sarah's blog gained traction, she caught the attention of a local nonprofit organization. They recognized her passion and invited her to speak at their annual event. Sarah stood on that stage, looking at a sea of faces despite her nerves. She realized she could inspire others with her story and dreams at that moment.

From that day forward, Sarah set her sights higher. She reached out to mentors, sought out scholarship opportunities, and pushed through the obstacles that once seemed impossible. With unwavering determination and belief in her power, she pursued her dreams of becoming an advocate for education in underprivileged communities.

Sarah's journey was far from easy, but she persisted, knowing that her potential knew no bounds. She knew that she had the power to overcome her circumstances and create a ripple of change that would extend far beyond her own life.

So, remember you are powerful, just like Sarah. You can rise above the odds and achieve greatness. It doesn't matter where you come from or what challenges you face. Embrace your dreams, believe in yourself, and never underestimate the impact you can have on the world. Your potential is waiting to shine, so go out there and show the world who you are and what you can do!

What are your thoughts about this scenario?

_____

_____

_____

_____

_____

_____

_____

I AM MADE TO BE MORE

I am fearfully and wonderfully made.
To do good works that won't fade;
To show more excellence in all I do;
To have more success in all I pursue;
To give more time to those in need;
To do more for others in word and deed;
To love more and be selfless;
To strive for more and obtain the best.
I am made for more prosperity.
I am made for the greatness God's planned for me.
In the future, there's a lot in store.
For I have a purpose. I am made to be more.

I am made to be more

A GIRL'S GUIDE TO BEING GREAT

2

EMBRACING YOUR UNIQUENESS

*"One of the lessons I grew up with was always to stay true to
yourself and never let what somebody else says distract you
from your goals. And so when I hear about negative and false
attacks, I don't invest any energy in them because I know who
I am."*
~First Lady Michelle Obama

How do you feel about yourself? Are you overly critical of
yourself? Do you diet because someone said you are
overweight or wear lots of makeup to hide your blemishes?

Let's talk about body image and self-esteem because they
affect everyone. So what's the difference? Here's the deal:
body image is how you see and feel about your body, while
self-esteem is how you feel about yourself. Here's the catch:
they're connected but not the same thing.

> Every one's body is unique and beautiful in their own way, including yours.

Body image is influenced by society,
media, and those annoying comparisons
we make with others. It's easy to get
caught up in the idea of a "perfect" body,
but here's the truth: there's no such
thing! Everyone's body is unique and
beautiful in their way, including yours.

Self-esteem, on the other hand, is all about how you value
yourself *beyond* your appearance. It's about recognizing your
strengths, talents, and inner beauty. When you have healthy
self-esteem, you love and accept yourself for who you are,
inside and out.

Meet Tracy. When Tracy was in middle school, her classmates teased her because she talked "differently." Tracy had a slight speech disorder that made her sound like she had an accent from another country.

When I met Tracy, she strolled with her shoulders humped forward and her head held down. She barely made eye contact with me. Tracy was only thirteen years old, but the sadness on her face made her look much older. She wore bandages on her fingernails, not as a new fashion statement, but to prevent her from biting her nails when she felt nervous about going to school. Can you imagine? Even though Tracy was an honor student, she did not look capable of doing well in school.

My heart broke for Tracy, and I had mixed emotions. I wanted so badly to let her know that it didn't matter what the students said about her, but I knew that it mattered to Tracy. I also felt anger towards the girls at school who thought it was okay to tease her, not knowing or caring about its effect on her. So I decided to spend time with Tracy and ask her about her experience at school.

As I listened, I encouraged her and gave her a much-needed heart-to-heart pep-talk. She left my office feeling better and looking confident. Tracy's self-esteem had improved! Her walk had changed (now she stood straight up), and she engaged me in conversation, smiled, and even laughed! I could see a tremendous difference in her. Tracy appeared to believe in herself for a few minutes, and it showed!

If you believe in yourself, others will likely trust you, too! Don't listen to haters. People who are insecure about themselves are usually the ones who talk about others. So don't take it personally. Instead, have the mindset of First Lady Michelle Obama when she said, "...I know who I am." Then accept it and own it!

Point to Ponder

How could Tracy improve her low self-esteem?

_____

_____

1. You Become What You Think You Are

It is wise to think positively about yourself because your actions follow your thoughts. For example, when I enrolled in college after I had been out of high school for many years, I had to take Math, which was not my favorite subject. I could not understand why I had to put letters with numbers, as we do in Algebra. How did this apply to real life anyway? Couldn't we do addition and subtraction and be done?

But since I had to take college-level Algebra, I decided to learn it and even *like* it! So I told myself I was brilliant and changed my thoughts about Math. I was determined not to be intimidated.

Because I *believed* I was smart, I *acted* that way by studying often and asking for help. As a result, I got an "A" in Algebra! I became what I said I was: smart! I realized I had everything I needed to do well in the class – faith, fortitude, focus, and the ability to think and comprehend, but I doubted myself.

However, when I deliberately *decided* that I was smart and my actions followed, the fear and self-doubt left. As a result, I got excellent grades. And I realized that once I made my mind up to do something, I could do it and do it very well.

I believe you can also.

Like me, train your brain to think good about yourself. Tell yourself that you are smart. Then act like it. Tell yourself that you make good decisions and make them. If there is something that you want to do and you don't think you can do it, change your thoughts. Then, take the steps to get it done.

Visualize yourself accomplishing your goals: finishing school, traveling the world, writing your bestseller book, or becoming the entrepreneur you want to become!

> If there is something that you want to do and you don't think you can do it, change your thoughts. Then take the steps to get it done.

Point to Ponder
How do your thoughts relate to accomplishing your goals?

_____

_____

2. Don't Compare

How often do you see someone and compare yourself to that person? Maybe it's a girl in your class or on television. Perhaps it's your friend or a cousin.

In my teens, I compared myself to other girls, fashionable and pretty, and sometimes was even envious of them – they got attention from boys, wore nice clothes, and seemed to have it together.

But now that I am older and wiser, I realize I wasted precious time thinking about them. I gave them more credit than they deserved. My more intelligent self knows that popularity doesn't last. Nor does it demonstrate a person's character (which is what matters most). I also learned that outside beauty fades with time, so I am glad I had a beautiful heart and spirit back then, which has remained with me throughout my adult years.

Comparing yourself (your hair, weight, athletic ability, etc.) to someone else is unrealistic because you are different. People have distinct looks, personalities, and styles from others. But that's a good thing. After all, the world would be incredibly dull if everyone looked and behaved the same way.

I also learned that outside beauty fades with time, so I am glad I had a beautiful heart and spirit back then, which has remained with me throughout my adult years.

Comparing yourself to someone else is like comparing bananas and pears. They are both fruits, but they are not the same. They don't look alike, nor should they. If bananas were exactly like pears, they would not be bananas. In the same way, if you had someone else's talents, complexion, or hair, you would not be *you.*

Another reason you should not compare yourself to others is that it is unfair to you to do so. When you compare yourself to someone else, you measure yourself against that person. As a result, you might try to change your personality or appearance to be like her, or you may feel inferior to her. This false standard of comparison is like telling yourself repeatedly that you don't like *you.* Eventually, you might begin to dislike yourself, try to gain others' approval, or even allow others to mistreat you.

You are better than that. So be kind to yourself. Accept, appreciate, and embrace your uniqueness. Remember that you are an original work of art! Therefore, don't apologize for who you are.

Point to Ponder
Should you strive to be famous? Why or why not?

_____

_____

3: Be Your Own Best Friend
Who's your "BFF" (Best Friend Forever)? What is the difference between a friend and a "best friend?" Do you have more than one best friend? In social media, sometimes total strangers request to be your friend. In this case, this is not a _true_ friend.

A true friend is someone with whom you are emotionally close. That person cares about you, is there for you when you need her, and defends or supports you even when you make a mistake.

> Accept, appreciate, and embrace your own uniqueness. Remember that you are an original work of art!

A _best_ friend is usually one person among your other friends with whom you have the closest and most profound relationship. You defend your best friend, protect her, and support her goals. So decide to be your best friend. For example, just like you accept your best friend with all her faults, appreciate yourself for who you are. In the same way, you don't judge your friend, don't judge yourself, or be too harsh on yourself. When you are _your_ best friend, you show others you love and respect yourself.

Point to Ponder
What can you do today to be your best friend?

_____

_____

Affirmation
Today, I decide to love myself just like I am, not to compare myself with anyone else, and give myself an "atta-girl."

I Am A

Creative
Beautiful
smart
valuable Loved worthy

WORK OF ART

A GIRL'S GUIDE TO BEING GREAT

Reflect and Write

1. How we see ourselves relates to our self-esteem. On the left side, write down three positive adjectives that describe your personality. For example, I am caring. On the other side, write down three positive physical traits you like about yourself, such as "my smile."

PERSONALITY TRAITS | PHYSICAL TRAITS

1._____ 1. _____

2._____ 2. _____

3. _____ 3. _____

2. Write an acrostic poem using the letters in your first name. Next to each letter, write a positive adjective that describes you. For example, KIM.

K – Kind
I – Important
M – Magnificent

3. What is the difference between high self-esteem and low self-esteem?

_____

_____

_____

_____

_____

4. How does it make you feel when you make wise choices for yourself? Why?

_____

_____

_____

_____

_____

5. How does it make you feel when you make poor choices for yourself? Why?

_____

_____

_____

_____

_____

6. Write a positive statement about yourself.

_____

_____

_____

_____

_____

Bonus Scenario for Embracing Your Uniqueness

It's a typical Monday morning at Westwood High School, where teenage girls in their sophomore year, Amy, Sharon, and Mia, prepare for another day of classes. The hallways buzz with excitement as students reconnect after the weekend. Among them, body image concerns weigh heavily on their minds.

Amy, a vibrant and athletic girl, often feels self-conscious about her muscular build. As she ties her sneakers in the locker room, she overhears a group of girls comparing themselves to celebrities, discussing their desire for thin, slender figures. Amy silently wonders if her muscular physique is "feminine" enough, as societal pressures tend to highlight a more delicate and petite body type.

Sharon, a creative soul with a quirky sense of style, stands in front of her mirror, observing her unique body shape. She loves experimenting with fashion and expressing herself through vibrant colors. However, Sharon often feels critical stares from peers who disagree with her style. Today, she decided to rock her outfit with confidence.

Meanwhile, a talented artist, Mia, flips through a fashion magazine, absorbed in the glossy images of seemingly perfect models. She yearns to possess flawless skin, slim waistlines, and symmetrical features. She sees her reflection and frowns, noticing the tiny blemishes on her face. The unrealistic beauty standards portrayed in the media leave Mia questioning her worth and feeling like she falls short of society's ideals.

Unbeknownst to these three girls, something extraordinary is about to happen. The school's administration has organized a body positivity workshop led by guest speakers promoting self-acceptance and embracing individuality. The workshop aims to challenge conventional beauty standards and create a supportive environment for all students.

As the morning progresses, the girls sit beside them in the school auditorium, surrounded by their peers. The guest speakers, individuals who have triumphed over body image struggles, share their personal stories, highlighting the damaging effects of societal pressures and the importance of self-love.

Moved by the speakers' experiences, the students engage in open and honest discussions. Amy realizes that her muscular build reflects her strength and athleticism, which she should embrace wholeheartedly. Sharon discovers that her unique style sets her apart, making her a trendsetter rather than an outcast. Mia recognizes that true beauty lies in her passion and creativity rather than conforming to an airbrushed ideal.

Inspired, the girls and their peers pledge to support one another in their journeys toward self-acceptance. They created a student-led body positivity club where they can openly discuss their struggles, celebrate their victories, and educate others about the importance of embracing diverse body types.

Over time, the club becomes a haven for girls struggling with body image issues. They organize empowering events, such as fashion shows featuring models of all shapes and sizes, art exhibitions celebrating different body forms, and panel discussions on media literacy and its impact on self-esteem. The movement grows beyond the school, influencing local communities and inspiring girls to love and accept themselves unconditionally.

Through the power of empathy, education, and solidarity, Amy, Sharon Mia, and their peers rewrite the narrative surrounding body image in their high school. They pave the way for future generations of young women to embrace their individuality, reject harmful beauty standards, and celebrate their bodies for the unique vessels of life and strength that they are.

What are your thoughts about this scenario?

_____

_____

_____

_____

_____

_____

_____

_____

_____

_____

_____

_____

_____

_____

_____

_____

_____

I am BEAUTIFULLY Exquisitely DESIGNED

I LOVE ME

I love me with skinny legs and all,
For it is these legs that have helped me climb
The ladder of success.
Will I appeal to someone any less?

I love me with my tiny little nose.
For it is this nose that has smelled the rain
Before it fell upon the earth.
After all, what is a pointy nose worth?

I love me with all my flaws.
For my flaws remind me that I'm unique,
So, no one's approval will I seek.

I love me with my curly hair.
For it is this hair that can be braided, platted,
Pinned up or worn in a fro.
Why did the texture of my hair once bother me so?

Yes, I am definitely different, uniquely me.
I'm masterfully created, wholeheartedly free!
When you gaze my way, what do you see?

I can accept the person within.
Where only a few have been.
Are you my enemy or my friend?

The friend, the mirror, that when I gaze its way;
Reaffirms that I'm okay.
And that when my outer appearance fade
I am still wonderfully and fearfully made!

Though you might laugh or disagree,
I am all I am, but not all I will be,
Because I've learned to love myself unashamedly.
Yes, I love me to the nth degree!

What is it about you that you haven't embraced?
Your small lips, wide hips, light skin, dark face?
Your walk, your talk, your personality?
When you look in the mirror, do you love what you see?
Or is it someone else that you long to be?

Don't dare compare yourself to me,
Your friends, or even a celebrity.
For the people you see in videos or on TV
are not all that they're made out to be.

So be true to you. To yourself, be true.
Let no one define or undermine you.
Love yourself with all your heart.
Because you are a work of art.

3

HONORING YOUR PRINCIPLES

By Darius Anthony and Rhonda G. Mincey

"If you don't stand for something, you'll fall for anything."
~Unknown

Let's discuss something super important: the courage to stand up for your principles, values, and standards. It might sound daunting, but trust me, it's a game-changer.

> Honoring your principles means staying true to who you are, even when it's not the popular choice.

Imagine this: you're in a situation where your friends pressure you to do something against your beliefs. Maybe it's skipping school or gossiping about someone. It's tempting to go along with the crowd, right? But here's the thing: honoring your principles means staying true to who you are, even when it's not the popular choice.

Let's break it down. Your principles are like your personal rulebook, the values and standards you hold dear. It could be treating others with kindness and honesty or standing up against injustice. When you stand up for what's right, you show the world that you won't compromise your values to fit in.

Now, I get it. It can be challenging to go against the flow. Taking a stand might mean having uncomfortable conversations, facing criticism, or losing friends. But here's the secret: when you stay true to your principles, you attract like-minded people who respect and admire your integrity. Unlike what social media tells us, quality means more than quantity.

> When you stay true to your principles, you attract like-minded people who respect and admire your integrity.

It's important to understand that standing up for what's right doesn't mean being judgmental or forcing your beliefs on others. It's about respectfully expressing your views, being open to different perspectives, and encouraging a positive change in your community.

So let's take a close look at values and standards. *Values* are the beliefs and principles we hold dear, while *standards* are the expectations and rules we set for ourselves and others. Values guide us in making decisions and behaving in ways that align with what matters most. While standards help us evaluate how well we or others meet those expectations.

For example, if honesty is a value you hold, you believe in telling the truth and being sincere. As a result, you might set a high standard for yourself to always be honest in your words and actions, meaning you expect yourself to be truthful even when it's challenging.

Values can vary between individuals and cultures, reflecting different priorities and beliefs.

Some common examples of values include:

- ❖ **Honesty:** Being truthful and trustworthy in our interactions with others.
- ❖ **Respect:** Treating others with dignity, regardless of differences.
- ❖ **Integrity**: Acting with moral and ethical principles.

- ❖ **Responsibility:** Being accountable for our actions and their consequences.
- ❖ **Compassion:** Showing empathy and care for the well-being of others.
- ❖ **Equality:** Believing in fair treatment and equal opportunities for all.
- ❖ **Freedom:** Valuing individual liberties and the right to make choices.
- ❖ **Justice:** Seeking fairness and equality in social and legal systems.
- ❖ **Sustainability**: Promoting the preservation and well-being of the environment.
- ❖ **Education:** Valuing knowledge, learning, and personal growth.

Point to Ponder
Which two values speak to you most?

_____

_____

1. Honor Your Values at All Times
Now that you've identified your top values let's explore why it's a good idea to stay true to them.

Let's look at Steven as an example. Steven was a bright and intelligent individual. He was well-known around his school as the "Smart Guy." Not only was he smart, but he was very athletic. He played basketball, baseball, and football. Since his ninth-grade year, he was swamped by girls who wanted to date him—you know, he was the typical athlete that we see in the movies and probably at your local school.

Steven made it to his eleventh-grade year with no problems, but suddenly, he started to slack in his work. He would barely do his homework and skipped his Trig class to hang out with friends. Steven did not care because he knew he was smart enough to get by without going to class. His parents had always taught him to go to school daily, do his homework, and maximize his time, but Steven had changed.

Steven's fame got to his head. He decided to do what pleased him because he was Steven, "The Smart Guy." But one day, when Stephen cut class, his teacher gave a pop quiz – those quizzes that none of us likes! Steven's teacher would not let him make up the exam because she did not excuse his absence. Remember, Steven didn't come to class. As a result, he received a zero for that quiz, and his coach suspended him from two football games!

His suspension hurt him more than receiving the zero because Steven loved sports, especially football. It was his life, but his coach stated that he would not tolerate any of his student-athletes skipping class and still being able to play in the games. No exemptions or exceptions! Since Steven was one of the best players on the team, his coach was not happy to sit him out, but he meant what he said, teaching Steven a lesson he would never forget.

From that time forward, Steven decided to always stick to his values and standards and not allow his "friends" or his conceit to steer him wrong. He had to stand up to them and let them know his education was more important than their friendship. He also had to take a stand and say he would not be easily persuaded because he is well-known.

As you can see, Steven compromised his values and lowered the standards his parents taught him. Even so, he recognized his mistake and vowed not to do that again.

When you honor your values, you become a stronger, more authentic individual who stays true to yourself and whom others admire.

Point to Ponder

Why is it important to always remember your values?

_____

_____

2. Recognize Your Mistakes

It takes a big person to recognize that they made a mistake. You can never go back and undo an error after you made it, but you can learn from it, apologize if necessary, and avoid repeating it. That is taking a stand.

> Take a stand for what you value! Stand up, hold your head up high, and declare that you will not lower your standards and compromise your values again.

Taking a stand is not limited to just talking. It could also be by a change of action, which in some circumstances is more important than speaking out about an issue. A person's words are meaningless without action to support them.

If you have ever compromised your values, do not feel bad because you are not the only one. Just do better.

Now that you know better, you can say, "Not another time will I compromise my values and lower my standards," which is what Steven did, as mentioned earlier in this chapter. Steven recognized he messed up and suffered consequences—failing the quiz. But he still admitted his mistakes.

It might not feel good to admit you made a poor decision, but this admission demonstrates your self-awareness and helps you move forward.

Point to Ponder
How do you move on after you have compromised your standards?

_____

_____

3. Set Your Standards Early
Early in life, deciding what you value and will stand for and against is wise. Then, when it's time for you to make decisions, it will be easier to know what is best for you, even if you don't always do it.

Standards are like traffic rules. If drivers do not have to obey the laws of the road, they can run red lights, drive without their seatbelt, and park wherever they want. This conduct could lead to people getting in accidents, engaging in road rage, or even getting seriously hurt. Therefore, the "rules of the road" are in place to guide drivers on where they can and cannot go and what they can and cannot do while driving.

Likewise, your standards should guide and protect you. But if you haven't decided what you stand for, you will have no pre-determined standard to help you make a sound decision when that time comes. As a result, you will probably not make the _best_ decision for you at that moment.

For example, suppose you decide it's non-negotiable for someone to respect you, and they talk harshly to you in front of others. Or someone hits you.

You will know that these behaviors are unacceptable in these cases, and you can quickly deal with them.

Sadly, I've seen so many girls who will date any guy who says what they want to hear even though he does not have a job, a high school education, or has several girlfriends. Make up your mind now that this will not be you.

Please do not lower your standards to meet someone else's low standards. Instead, make that person meet your high standards. Don't waste your time and energy trying to change someone and reacting emotionally. You're worth more than that!

> Please do not lower your standards to meet someone else's low standards. Instead, make that person meet your high standards.

Set high standards today about what you will and will not allow.

Here are nine ways to help you set high standards:

❖ **Define your values**: Reflect on your values and what matters most. Identify the qualities and principles that you want to embody in your life. This self-awareness will provide a foundation for setting high standards aligned with your beliefs.

❖ **Set specific goals**: Identify what goals you want to accomplish in various aspects of your life, such as academics, extracurricular activities, personal growth, and relationships. Then, break them down into smaller steps and milestones. Next, write your action plan to achieve them.

❖ **Challenge yourself:** Go beyond your limits and take on new challenges. Seek opportunities that require effort and growth. You can constantly challenge yourself to expand your skills, knowledge, and capabilities.

❖ **Get around positive people:** Surround yourself with people who inspire and motivate you. For instance, seek mentors, role models, and friends who share your aspirations and encourage you to reach higher. Their support and guidance can be invaluable in setting and maintaining high standards.

❖ **Develop self-discipline:** Cultivate self-discipline to stay focused and committed to your goals, for example, minimizing distractions and maintaining a solid work ethic. Consistency and perseverance are key.

❖ **Embrace failure as a growth opportunity:** Failing lets you know what isn't working. So instead of being discouraged, view your obstacles as opportunities and setbacks as solutions. Reevaluate, readjust, refresh, and reset.

❖ **Practice self-care:** Setting high standards doesn't mean neglecting your well-being. Prioritize activities that nourish and recharge you, such as exercise, hobbies, spending time with loved ones, and being present.

❖ **Seek continuous improvement:** Embrace a mindset of constant improvement. Strive to enhance your knowledge, skills, and abilities in all areas of your life. Look for ways to learn, whether it's through formal education, self-study, or seeking out new experiences.

❖ **Celebrate achievements:** Acknowledge and celebrate your accomplishments, no matter how small they may seem. Recognize your progress and the effort you put into reaching your goals. Celebrating achievements can reinforce the importance of high standards and motivate you to keep striving for excellence.

Remember that setting high standards is not about perfectionism or comparing yourself to others. It's about challenging yourself to become the best version of yourself and living in alignment with your values. Be kind to yourself along the journey and enjoy the process of growth and self-discovery.

So, here's your call to action. Be brave, be bold, and honor your principles.

> Remember that setting high standards is not about perfectionism or comparing yourself to others. It's about challenging yourself to become the best version of yourself and living in alignment with your values.

Point to Ponder
Why is it important to set high standards for yourself now?

_____

_____

Affirmation
From now on, I declare I will take a stand to protect my values and standards.

ASPIRE TO GO HIGHER

Reflect and Write

1. What do you value? For example, having integrity (not cheating, lying, and keeping your word) or good grades.

_____

_____

_____

_____

2. Is it difficult to have friends who don't value what you value? Why or why not?

_____

_____

_____

_____

3. What advice would you give someone needing help standing up for what they believe in?

_____

_____

_____

_____

4. Has there been a time when you lowered your standards? How did that make you feel? What did you learn?

_____

_____

_____

_____

I am the Author of my own Story

A Girl's Guide to Being Great

Bonus Scenario for Honoring Your Principles

Jacqueline, a passionate environmentalist, has always cared deeply about the environment. She volunteers at a local conservation organization, participates in beach clean-ups, and actively promotes recycling and reducing waste in her community. Jacqueline often encourages her friends and family to adopt eco-friendly practices and educates them about the environmental consequences of their actions.

On the other hand, Karen, a high school senior, had just returned from a summer trip where she witnessed communities without clean drinking water. It hit her hard. Back home, she discovers that her school's water fountains had lead levels way above safe limits. "Not on my watch," she thinks. Rallying her classmates, she organizes a "Water Walk" event, where students carry jugs around the track to symbolize the daily struggle many face. With the funds raised and the attention garnered, Karen pushes the school board to address the water issue. For Karen, it isn't just about hydration but justice.

As they go through high school, Jacqueline and Karen often talk deeply about their values, sharing their perspectives and learning from each other. They attend rallies and events, combining their passions and fighting for causes that intersect with their interests, such as environmental justice.

Their shared passion for making a difference in the world leads Jacqueline and Karen to organize a joint initiative at their high school. They started an environmental and social justice club to educate their peers about how these issues are alike. Through workshops, film screenings, and guest speakers, they inspire fellow students to reflect on their values and take action to address the pressing challenges facing their community and the world.

Jacqueline and Karen's friendship becomes a source of support and encouragement as they face challenges and setbacks. They navigate conflicts and differing opinions with respect and empathy, recognizing that their unique perspectives contribute to their growth and understanding. Their shared values create a strong foundation for their friendship, allowing them to grow while supporting each other's endeavors.

Throughout their teenage years, Jacqueline and Karen's values continue to evolve and shape their lives. They inspire others with dedication, becoming role models within their school and community. Their friendship is a reminder that when people come together, driven by their values and a shared vision, they can impact the world around them.

What are your thoughts about this scenario?

_____

_____

_____

_____

_____

_____

_____

STAND STRONG

Though peer pressure surrounds me everywhere I turn
And temptation's all around me; there's a lesson to learn;

I can stand on my own and not follow the crowd;
I can make my own decisions and make myself proud.

I can say "NO" to things that are not good for me
And not worry about my status or popularity.

I can walk away before trouble begins
And listen to the voice within.

For, if other people's standards are lower than mine
I will leave them alone, and I'll be just fine.

And if our values do not match,
I can walk away gladly without looking back.

Because I know that what is in me
It is more than they care to see.
The truth is that my values belong to me.

And when people try to degrade or persuade me,
I know they didn't make me, nor can they shake me.

So I will stand against what is wrong
Because I know I am not alone.

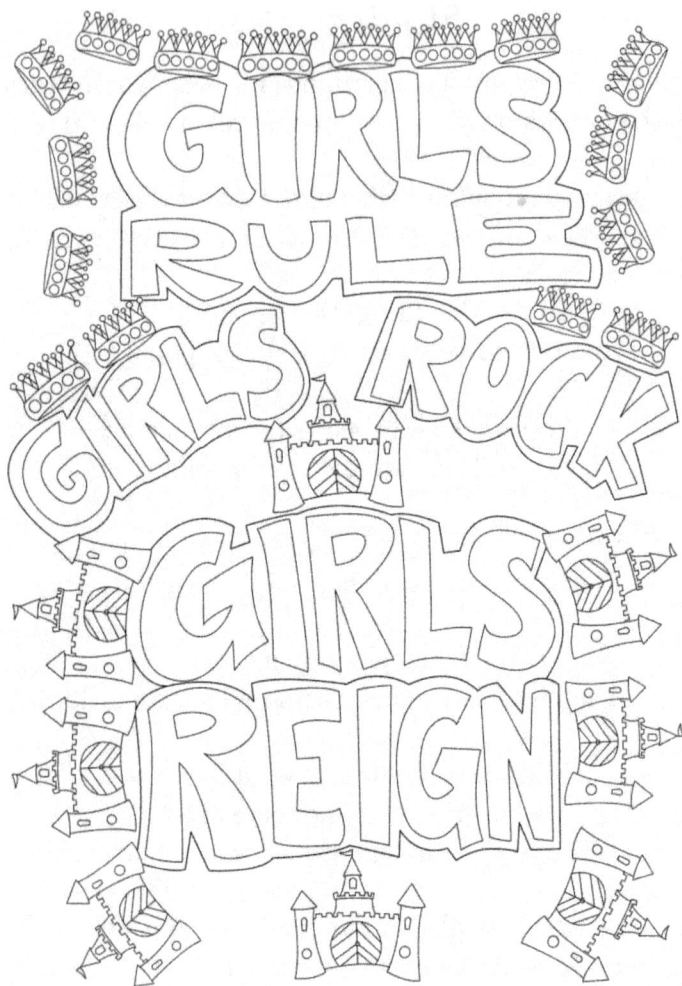

GIRLS RULE
GIRLS ROCK
GIRLS REIGN

A Girl's Guide to Being Great

4

NAVIGATING LIFE'S CROSSROADS

"Somewhere along the line of development, we discover what we really are, and then we make our real decision for which we are responsible. Make that decision primarily for yourself because you can never really live anyone else's life, not even your child's."
~ Eleanor Roosevelt (1884 - 1962)
Former First Lady of the United States

Life has this funny way of throwing us curveballs and leading us to a crossroads where we must decide which road to take. You know those moments when you're scratching your head and thinking, "What in the world do I do now?"

In this chapter, we're diving into the art of decision-making and problem-solving. We'll explore how to handle those moments when you're faced with tough choices and are unsure which path to take.

Imagine this: Someone invited you to two fantastic events on the same night. On the one hand, there's a concert of your favorite band that you've been dying to see live. On the other hand, your best friend's birthday party is also taking place, and she means the world to you.

Now, you're at a crossroads. Do you follow your heart's desire and rock out at the concert, or prioritize your friendship and celebrate with your bestie? It's one of those moments when you wish life came with an instruction manual to give you answers.

Every day, you make many decisions. Some of your decisions are so small that you might not realize that you are making decisions. In contrast, other decisions you make require more thought and time.

Every day, you make many decisions. Some of your choices are so small that you might not realize you are making decisions. In contrast, other choices you make require more thought and time.

For example, did you brush your teeth today or put on deodorant? If so, you probably didn't put much thought into that. On the other hand, considering what job to take would require more review and time.

Other decisions you might make are: How will you do your hair? How long should you study? Should you get a tattoo? And the list goes on.

However, one of the most important decisions that you will make is who you let in your inner circle. You know, those ride-or-die friends who have your back no matter what. But here's the thing: not everyone deserves a VIP pass to your life.

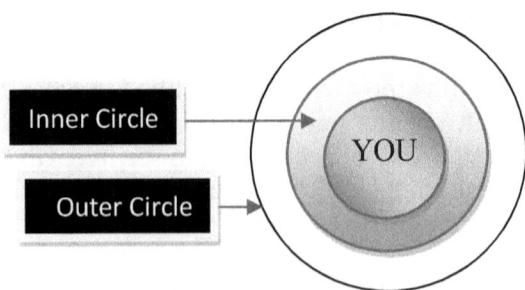

Picture this: You've met someone new at school, and they seem pretty cool at first. They're funny and stylish, and everyone seems to like them. But you notice some red flags as you spend more time with them. They're always gossiping about others, and you catch them spreading rumors about people behind their backs.

Now, you're standing at a crossroads. Do you brush off their behavior and continue hanging out with them because they're famous? Or do you trust your gut and distance yourself from someone who doesn't align with your values?

Again, choosing who gets to be in your inner circle is a big deal. These people influence your thoughts, actions, and overall vibe. So, let's look at how to handle this situation.

First things first, trust your instincts. If something feels off about a person, don't ignore it. Your gut can pick up on things your mind might not catch immediately. It's like your own personal built-in lie detector.

Second, pay attention to how they treat others. Actions speak louder than words, my friend. If someone consistently disrespects or behaves in ways that go against your values, it's a clear sign that they might not be the best fit for your inner circle.

> Surround yourself with friends who uplift you, inspire you, and push you to be the best version of yourself. Remember, your vibe attracts your tribe.

Third, consider the long-term impact. Think about the kind of person you want to become. Surround yourself with friends who uplift you, inspire you, and push you to be the best version of yourself. Remember, your vibe attracts your tribe.

Lastly, don't be afraid to let go. If you realize that someone isn't a positive influence or brings unnecessary drama into your life, it's okay to distance yourself. It's not about being mean or judgmental; it's about taking care of yourself and surrounding yourself with people who genuinely care about your well-being.

Point to Ponder
List two traits that people in your inner circle should have:

_____

_____

1. Today's Decisions Will Affect Your Future

Let's talk about something that might seem far away but is super important: your future. Yep, the choices you make today can significantly impact what lies ahead. So, let's dive into how your decisions today can shape your future, especially when choosing the people in your inner circle.

Picture this: You're hanging out with friends who constantly encourage each other to skip classes, slack off on assignments, and prioritize partying over studying. It might seem fun and carefree, but let's fast-forward.

You're at a crossroads, facing college applications or career opportunities. Suddenly, you realize that your grades and work ethic have suffered because of the choices you made with your friends. Now you're thinking, "I wish I had surrounded myself with people who motivated me to reach my full potential."

Guess what? It's never too early to start making choices that align with your long-term goals.

Here's how:

First and foremost, take a moment to envision your ideal future. What kind of person do you want to become? What are your dreams and aspirations? This vision will help you make decisions that correspond with your goals.

Next, evaluate the impact of your current choices. Consider how the people you surround yourself with influence your behavior, mindset, and ambitions. Are they lifting you or holding you back? Choose friends who inspire and motivate you to be the best version of yourself.

Also, remember that it's okay to be selective. You don't have to be friends with everyone or follow the crowd if it doesn't resonate with who you are. Surround yourself with a few close friends who genuinely support and believe in you.

> *"Trust your instincts. If something feels off or doesn't sit right, listen to that inner voice."*
> *– Serena Williams*

Lastly, trust your instincts. If someone gives you a bad vibe or consistently engages in behaviors that go against your values, it's time to reevaluate their place in your close circle. Listen to that inner voice telling you what feels right and what doesn't.

So, beautiful young lady, as you make choices today, think about how they can impact your future.

For example, after graduating high school, I enrolled in college but didn't finish. Instead, I chose to start my own business. But many years later, at 45, I re-enrolled in college and graduated with top honors. At 50, I earned my master's, graduating Summa Cum Laude. Because of this, I became a college professor, made life-long connections, and developed a strong work ethic that carries me far in my business.

Remember, your future is bright, and your decisions can shape it into something extraordinary. Trust yourself, follow your dreams, and rock that future like the superstar you are!

Point to Ponder
Why is it important to make good decisions today?

_____

_____

2. Every Decision Has Consequences

Every choice you make, big or small, has consequences. It's like throwing a pebble into a pond and watching the ripples spread.

Let's start with school. Imagine you're faced with a decision to study for that upcoming test or spend the entire night binge-watching your favorite show. In the short term, staying up all night might seem like a blast, but the next day, you're sleep-deprived, struggling to focus, and your test performance suffers. Ouch!

Now, fast forward to the long term. Those study habits you develop, or lack thereof, can affect your grades, college opportunities, and even career prospects down the line. It's not just about that one test—it's about the skills and discipline you cultivate through consistent choices.

But wait, decision-making and the consequences don't stop at school. Let's look at choices outside of the classroom, too. Say someone invites you to a party where you know there might be some sketchy activities going on. You have a decision: attend and risk getting involved in something uncomfortable, or politely decline and maintain your integrity.

In the short term, going to the party might seem exciting and like a chance to fit in. However, in the long term, your decision could impact your reputation, relationships, and even your safety. Staying true to yourself and making choices that come in agreement with your values can lead to more positive outcomes in the future.

Every decision about school, friendships, or personal choices affects your life. It's like connecting the dots, each representing a decision, and the lines between them trace your journey.

> Every decision about school, friendships, or personal choices, affects your life. It's like connecting the dots, each representing a decision, and the lines between them trace your journey.

So, take a moment to consider the consequences of your choices. Reflect on the short-term and long-term impact they can have. Will that decision help you grow, learn, and move closer to your goals? Or will it hold you back, create unnecessary obstacles, or lead you down a path you don't want go go?

Remember, you're in the driver's seat of your life. Embrace the power of thoughtful decision-making and let your choices' ripples create a future full of opportunities, growth, and fulfillment.

You've got this, and your future is waiting for you to shape it with every decision.

Point to Ponder
List a positive consequence of a decision you made.

_____

_____

3. Some Decisions are Life-Changing
The power to shape your destiny knows no boundaries, whether in a traditional school, homeschooling, or pursuing a non-traditional path.

First up, let's talk about traditional school settings. Suppose you're faced with choosing to join a sports team or extracurricular club. Maybe it's basketball, theater, or a coding club—whatever rocks your world. Getting involved in activities outside the class can introduce you to new passions, develop your skills, and create lifelong friendships. It's a decision that can shape your social life, build character, and open doors to future opportunities.

Now, let's shift our focus to homeschooled girls. One life-changing decision could be exploring online courses or joining virtual communities to enhance your learning experience. For instance, taking coding classes on platforms like Khan Academy or joining online forums to connect with like-minded individuals can expand your knowledge and skills in exciting ways. It's about seizing the opportunity to carve your educational path and tapping into resources beyond traditional classroom walls.

But wait, life-changing decisions aren't just about academics. Let's dive into choices outside of school, too. Imagine you have a passion for entrepreneurship or starting a business. You're at a fork in the road. Do you follow the traditional path of finding a job or leap into building your venture? This decision can be life-changing because it allows you to shape your career, chase your dreams, and create your success story. It's about embracing the unconventional and paving your unique path.

But let's say you go against your better judgment and take a left, although you believe it's best to go right. Let's look at Cynthia's story.

Cynthia has a pattern of making reckless decisions. For example, she had boyfriends who were abusive to her in middle school, and she cut classes in high school. Cynthia eventually graduated from high school and attended college but dropped out when she was nineteen to follow her much older boyfriend to another city. He lived in her apartment, but Cynthia paid the bills. Two years later, Cynthia became a mother. She had planned to go into the military but has had to rethink her plan because she now has a child.

Cynthia made several decisions, one after another that changed her life forever.

You, like Cynthia, will have to make many difficult decisions as a young lady. However, the consequences will be inevitable regardless of your reasons for making them.

> Sometimes we do not understand the full effect of our decisions until later in life when it is impossible to change the outcome.

And here's the deal: Sometimes, we do not understand the full effect of our decisions until later in life when it is impossible to change the outcome.

It can be as simple as deciding to volunteer for a cause you're passionate about, as significant as traveling solo to explore the world and broaden your horizons, or as stressful as caring for your baby as a single mom. So, intentionally make decisions that your future self will thank you for.

Point to Ponder
What is an example of a life-changing decision?
_____

_____

Affirmation
Today, I choose to make good decisions about what I do and who I am with because these decisions will affect my future.

A Girl's Guide to Being Great

Reflect and Write

1. Why is it difficult for some people to make wise decisions?

_____

_____

_____

_____

_____

2. Think about a different decision you'd make if you had the chance. If it isn't too personal, write it here.

_____

_____

_____

_____

_____

_____

3. Think about a decision that you are _glad_ you made. Explain.

_____

_____

_____

_____

_____

_____

4. The decisions you make can affect other people. List three people your choices will affect besides you.

_____

_____

_____

_____

_____

_____

5. What negative or positive consequences can result from the following decisions? Please list at least two.

a. Graduate from high school

_____

_____

b. Get a college degree (bachelor's, master's, or doctorate)

_____

_____

c. Lie to your parents

_____

_____

d. Disobey or disrespect people in authority

_____

_____

_____

e. Drop out of school

_____

_____

f. Date someone who verbally or physically abuses you

_____

_____

g. Bully someone

_____

_____

h. Drink alcohol (beer and liquor)

_____

_____

i. Exercise regularly

_____

_____

j. Demonstrate kindness to others

_____

_____

k. Smoke cigarettes and use tobacco or drugs

_____

_____

l. Start your own business

_____

_____

A Girl's Guide to Being Great

Bonus Scenario for Navigating Life's Crossroads

Sue Lin is a 16-year-old girl facing a common problem among teenagers: feeling overwhelmed by social media pressures. Sue Lin has noticed that spending time on social media platforms like Instagram and TikTok has negatively impacted her self-esteem and overall mental well-being. She constantly compares herself to her peers' seemingly perfect lives and appearances, leaving her feeling inadequate and anxious. Sue Lin wants to find a way to address this issue and regain her self-confidence.

Problem-solving Steps:

❖ **Self-Reflection and Awareness:** Sue Lin begins by reflecting on her feelings and social media's impact on her well-being. She acknowledges that comparing herself to others is harmful and wants to change.

❖ **Research and Education:** Sue Lin takes the initiative to research and educate herself on the effects of social media on mental health. She reads articles, watches videos, and listens to podcasts discussing social media's negative aspects and the importance of self-acceptance.

❖ **Seeking Support**: Recognizing that she's not alone in facing this issue, Sue Lin confides in her close friends about her concerns regarding social media pressures. They empathize with her and offer their support. They also share their experiences and insights, helping Sue Lin feel understood and less isolated.

❖ **Setting Boundaries**: Sue Lin establishes boundaries with social media to regain control over her emotions. She limits her daily usage and unfollows accounts that do not make her feel good. Instead, she seeks out those that promote body positivity, mental health awareness, and personal growth.

❖ **Building a Supportive Network:** Sue Lin connects with like-minded individuals through online communities, forums, or local support groups focusing on healthy social media habits and positive self-image. She participates in discussions, shares her experiences, and learns from others who have successfully overcome similar challenges.

❖ **Exploring Offline Activities:** To strike a balance between her online and offline life, Sue Lin starts exploring new hobbies and activities that she enjoys. She joins a dance class, volunteers at a local charity, and spends more time with her family and friends. These offline experiences helped her develop a stronger sense of identity and fulfillment beyond social media.

❖ **Practicing Self-Care and Mindfulness:** Sue Lin prioritizes self-care activities such as journaling, practicing mindfulness, and engaging in regular physical exercise. These practices help her to manage stress, improve her self-esteem, and cultivate a positive mindset.

❖ **Becoming an Advocate:** Feeling empowered by her personal growth, Sue Lin advocates for responsible social media usage among her peers. She starts a blog or creates social media content that promotes authenticity, self-acceptance, and mental well-being. She aims to inspire and support other teen girls struggling with similar issues by sharing her journey and providing tips.

Sue Lin successfully addresses her social media pressures through these problem-solving steps and learns to prioritize her mental health and self-worth. She becomes a role model for others, creating a positive impact in her community and helping girls navigate the challenges of the digital world.

What are your thoughts about this scenario?

_____

_____

_____

_____

_____

_____

_____

_____

_____

_____

_____

_____

_____

_____

_____

_____

I AM THE FACE OF GREATNESS™

A Girl's Guide to Being Great

CHOICES

Every choice I make has a consequence.
So when I choose, I use common sense.

I also must decide what is best for me.
And decide with accountability.

The results of my decisions can cause joy or pain.
So I have to ask: What will I lose or gain?

Who, besides me, will my decisions affect?
Will it give me a life of promise or one of regret?

The decisions I make today will affect tomorrow.
The consequence will lead to success or sorrow.

So I choose to be smart. I choose to work hard.
I choose to be my "best" me; of drugs, I'll have no part.

I choose to have a positive outlook and attitude.
I choose not to drink alcohol, which can alter my mood.

I chose not to smoke cigarettes to relieve my stress.
I choose to make A's and B's, not "just pass" a test.

I choose to refrain from any activity.
That compromises my standards and my purity.

When I decide to do something, whether it's right or wrong,
I must accept the consequences, for they are mine alone.

So, today I decide at this very hour.
To choose the *best* path for *me*, for only I have that power.

I Love the Life I Live
I Live the Life I Love

5
THRIVING UNDER PRESSURES

*"Be of good cheer. Do not think of today's failures, but of the
success that may come tomorrow. You have set yourselves a
difficult task, but you will succeed if you persevere;
and you will find a joy in overcoming obstacles.
Remember, no effort we make to attain something beautiful is
ever lost."*
~ Helen Keller (1880 - 1968)
Author, political activist, and lecturer

Life can sometimes feel like a pressure cooker, with
expectations and challenges coming at you from every
direction. But guess what? You have the power to withstand
those pressures and thrive amidst them. This chapter will
explore three essential points to help you rise above and
unleash your inner warrior. Prepare to conquer the
challenges and show the world what you're made of!

Pressure is like that annoying little voice telling you to be
perfect, to fit in, or to meet certain expectations. The weight
of comparison, judgment, and the fear of failure can
sometimes suffocate you. But here's the thing: pressure only
has power over you if you let it.

As a young girl, I experienced many of the pressures you now
experience; I wanted to fit in and be liked by others. However,
I resisted the pressure to use drugs or drink alcohol for several
reasons: I thought about what my mother would do to me if
she found out, I didn't want to disappoint my mother, and I
didn't want to start doing something that I believed could very
likely lead me down the wrong road.

So to help me deal with the pressures of being a teenager, I associated with two other girls who thought like me – girls who were *trying* to do the right thing. Even then, sometimes it was still not easy to resist the temptation to go places where we should not have gone or to stay out past curfew, which created an inner conflict.

Point to Ponder
List two people who help you handle pressures.

_____

_____

1. Embrace Your Inner Strength
When the pressure builds, it's time to tap into your inner strength. Picture it as your superpower, unique to you. Just like Wonder Woman, who faced seemingly insurmountable challenges but never backed down, you too possess that same resilience and power within you. Embrace, believe in it, and let it guide you through the most challenging times. Here's how:

❖ Take a deep breath and remind yourself of your accomplishments and strengths. Reflect on the challenges you have overcome before and draw inspiration from them.

❖ Surround yourself with positive influences, supportive friends, and mentors who believe in you. They will be your cheerleaders during tough times and help you find your strength when you feel like giving up.

❖ Practice self-compassion and treat yourself with kindness. Remember, you're only human, and it's okay to make mistakes. Be gentle with yourself and give yourself the love and care you deserve.

Point to Ponder
What's one way you can embrace your inner strength?

_____

_____

2. Shift Perspective and Embrace Growth

Instead of viewing pressure as a burden, reframe it as an opportunity for growth. Pressure can push you to discover your hidden potential, test your limits, and unveil strengths you never knew you had.

Look at the diamond: A diamond is usually given to someone on special occasions, such as an engagement, birthday, or wedding anniversary. A diamond also signifies love and importance and is said to be a "girl's best friend."

According to the Gemological Institute of America:

❖ Diamonds are virtually fireproof.
❖ Diamonds are the most durable gemstone on earth.
❖ Diamonds are formed approximately 100 miles from the earth's surface.
❖ Diamonds come to the earth's surface by being pushed through the ground through volcanic activity.

> You are tough, precious, desirable, valuable, brilliant, and unbreakable like a diamond! You rock, so let no one stop your shine!

Talk about pressure! But without that pushing movement, we would not be able to admire a diamond for its many qualities, and it would not be the symbol of love and prestige it represents.

Pressure makes you shine even through the most challenging circumstances and darkest places of your life in the same way that it brings out the brilliance in a diamond from the depths of the earth.

You are precious, desirable, valuable, brilliant, and unbreakable like a diamond! You rock, so let no one stop your shine! Here's how to do that:

- ❖ Embrace a growth mindset. Understand that setbacks and failures are not permanent. They are stepping stones on your path to success. Use them as opportunities to learn, adapt, and grow stronger.
- ❖ Embrace challenges as learning experiences. When faced with a difficult situation, ask yourself, "How can I use this experience to improve?" This shift in perspective can turn pressure into a catalyst for personal and skill development.
- ❖ Push beyond your comfort zone. Growth often happens when you push beyond what is familiar. Embrace new experiences, try new things, and embrace life outside your comfort zone.

Point to Ponder
How can pressure make you grow?

_____

_____

3. Cultivate Resilience and Self-Care
Resilience is your secret weapon when it comes to thriving under pressure. It's the ability to bounce back, adapt, and keep moving forward, even when things get tough. But remember, resilience goes hand in hand with self-care.

- ❖ Practice self-care routines that nourish your mind, body, and soul. Whether through exercise, mindfulness, hobbies, or simply spending time with loved ones, prioritize activities that recharge and rejuvenate you.

❖ Develop a support system. Surround yourself with positive influences and people who uplift and support you. Lean on them for guidance, advice, and encouragement when situations get tricky.

❖ Celebrate small victories along the way. Recognize and appreciate your progress, no matter how small it may seem. Each step forward is a testament to your strength and resilience.

❖ Next, use your voice. For example, say, "No." "No" isn't a dirty word. Saying "No" to your peers takes courage but can save you from terrible consequences.

> Celebrate small victories along the way. Recognize and appreciate your progress, no matter how small it may seem.

Remember this: People who try to persuade you to participate in behaviors you feel uncomfortable doing or know are wrong are not your friends. They do not have your best interest at heart, so you don't have to try to impress them. In a few years, you probably will not remember their names.

So if someone is pressuring you into doing activities and you are uncertain about what to do, ask these questions:

1. Does this decision align with my values?
2. Have I considered the consequences?
3. How will this decision affect my future?
4. How will this decision affect my family?
5. How will this decision affect my health?
6. How will this decision affect my reputation?

7. How will I feel about myself afterward?
8. Would I do this if my parents (or someone I respect) watched me?

In the face of pressure, remember that you have the power to succeed. Pressure is just a temporary cloud, but your inner warrior shines through. Embrace the challenges, learn and grow from them, and show the world your capabilities. You've got this, and nothing can stand in your way.

Point to Ponder
What question can you ask yourself if someone pressures you to do something that goes against your values?

_____

_____

_____

Affirmation
I will not give in to the weight of pressure because I have the strength to handle them.

Reflect and Remark

1. Do you ever put pressure on yourself by comparing yourself to others or by wanting to please others? Why or why not?

_____

_____

_____

_____

_____

_____

_____

_____

2. What pressures have you experienced as a daughter, friend, or student?

_____

_____

_____

_____

_____

_____

_____

_____

3. How do you deal with the pressures from Question 2? Is there a better way that you could handle them? Explain.

_____

_____

_____

_____

_____

_____

_____

_____

_____

_____

_____

4. Diamonds come from intense pressure. List several characteristics of diamonds that apply to you.

_____

_____

_____

_____

_____

_____

_____

Bonus Scenario for Thriving Under Pressures

Tina and Monica were best friends about to enter their final year of high school. As they prepared for this crucial phase of their lives, they faced immense pressure from various sources. Yet, they were determined to conquer these challenges together and emerge stronger.

First and foremost, academic expectations loomed over Tina and Monica like a dark cloud. College applications, standardized tests, and the pressure to achieve top grades weighed heavily on their minds. However, instead of giving in to stress, they supported each other. They formed a study group with like-minded classmates, sharing knowledge and motivating one another. Working together alleviated their anxieties, and they discovered that collaboration was vital to success.

Tina and Monica also faced social pressures. The expectations to fit in, conform to societal standards, and be popular were ever-present. They noticed how certain groups of girls were focused on external appearances and popularity, which created a toxic environment. Determined to rise above these pressures, Tina and Monica embraced their individuality. They pursued their passions, such as writing and painting, without worrying about societal judgment. Their authenticity and self-confidence attracted like-minded friends, creating a supportive circle and encouraging personal growth.

As their final year progressed, the girls faced another challenge: the fear of the unknown. They were uncertain about their future paths, careers, and what awaited them beyond high school. But instead of letting anxiety consume them, they embarked on a journey of exploration. They attended career fairs, spoke with professionals, and sought guidance from mentors. Through these experiences, they discovered their true passions and built a roadmap for their future endeavors.

Under these pressures, Tina and Monica realized their inner strength and resilience. They learned to prioritize their mental well-being and seek help when needed. They practiced self-care through regular exercise, meditation, and engaging in activities that brought them joy.

As the final year ended, Tina and Monica reflected on their journey. They realized that the pressures they faced were not insurmountable obstacles but stepping stones to personal growth. They emerged more confident, ready to face the challenges ahead.

Ultimately, Tina and Monica's story proves the power of friendship, resilience, and self-discovery. They overcame academic pressures, social expectations, and the fear of the unknown by supporting each other, embracing their individuality, and exploring their passions. Their journey inspires others to face their challenges and find the strength to overcome them.

What are your thoughts about this scenario?

_____

_____

_____

_____

_____

_____

_____

_____

PRESSURES

Make good grades. Try out for track.
Do my chores and do not slack.

Study for the C.R.C.T.
Go to college. Get my G.E.D.

History or Biology?
Why is my mom yelling at me?

Will he call me? Will I win?
Will I have to take this test again?

If he calls, what do I say?
When will this pimple go away?

Want to smoke? No, I'm good,
But yet I wonder if I should.

Should I tweet? Where should we meet?
A pop quiz! Should I cheat or try to compete?

Decisions. Pressures. Noise. Fuss.
How do I cope without getting crushed?

I feel overwhelmed, tired, and stressed.
Yet I try to do my best,
But how do I cope with life's daily demands?
Do you even understand?

A Girl's Guide to Being Great

6

Pursuing Your Dreams

"If you can dream it, you can do it. Always remember this thing was started by a mouse."
~Walt Disney (1901-1966)
Motion picture producer and the creator of Disneyland

Get ready to embark on a chapter about dreams and wishes and why having a vision is a game-changer. We often use "dream" and "wish" interchangeably, but let's dive deeper and understand the difference. This chapter explores the power of dreams, why they matter, and why every girl should have a dream.

> Dreams have the power to transform your life. Having a dream ignites a fire within you, propelling you forward and giving you purpose.

So, what's the difference between a dream and a wish? A wish is like throwing a coin into a fountain, hoping something magically happens. It's passive, like crossing your fingers and waiting for things to fall into place. But a dream is a whole different story. A dream is a burning desire deep within your soul. It's a vision of what you want to achieve, a map to guide you toward your wildest aspirations.

So why should you have a dream for your life? Here's the truth: dreams have the power to transform your life. Having a passion ignites a fire within you, propelling you forward and giving you purpose. Dreams shape your goals, inspire you to take action, and push you beyond what you thought was possible. Having a vision is like having a compass guiding your journey.

Sometimes, we might think dreams are only for the lucky few or the famous people we admire. But here's the secret: dreaming is for everyone, especially you!

Your dreams matter, and you have the power to bring them to life. So, let go of doubts or fears and embrace the magic of dreaming. It's time to unleash your inner dreamer, set your sights high, and prepare to take those significant steps toward your goals.

1. Dream Big!

When you have a dream for your life, you imagine yourself doing something. What is your goal for yourself? Is it running your own business? Is it conducting experiments? Or is it helping people around the world?

> **Keep going! Success is ahead.**

When you dream big, you have ambitious and aspirational goals for the future. It involves envisioning a life beyond your current circumstances, societal limitations, and stereotypes and setting your sights on achieving something meaningful.

> Your dream should be big! But people often dream small based on what they think is reasonable and possible.

Your dream should be big! But people often dream small based on what they think is reasonable and possible. However, the downside is that you limit yourself and hold back your potential to accomplish great things. It's all about your mindset.

What is the size of your dream? Is your dream the size of a saucer, paper plate, or pizza box?

When I wrote this book, I envisioned girls worldwide reading it. I dreamed of selling millions of copies and having them translated into different languages, including French and Spanish.

I've learned to take the limits off my dreams. And you know what? You should, too! After all, if you think small, you will probably obtain small successes, but if you think big, you can reach for and receive enormous, almost unimaginable successes!

Point to Ponder
Why should *you* dream big?

_____

_____

2. Embrace the Power of Possibilities
First, let go of those limitations and allow yourself to dream big. Remember, the sky's the limit! Just like Malala Yousafzai, who dreamed of an education for all girls and fought tirelessly to make it happen, you, too, have the power to make a difference and achieve extraordinary things.

Let's begin. Imagine your ideal future. Close your eyes and envision what you want to accomplish, who you want to become, and how you want to impact the world.

Write it down. Putting your dreams into words gives them power and helps you clarify your goals. Don't hold back. Dare to dream beyond what seems realistic or achievable. Let your imagination run wild, and believe in the power of your dreams!

Once you have a clear picture of your dreams, it's time to create a vision board. Think of it as a visual representation of your aspirations and a powerful tool for manifesting your desires. Let's get creative and make our dreams come to life!

You will need:

1 Posterboard
Scissors
Magazines
Glue sticks or tape
Paper or index cards
Markers or colored pencils

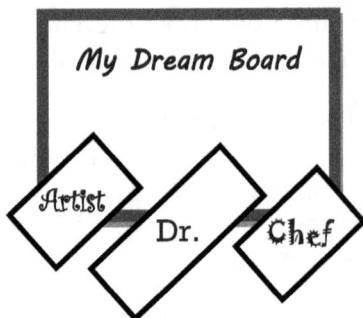

My Dream Board

Artist

Dr.

Chef

4 Steps to Making Your Dream Board

1. Visualize and write down what you'd like to accomplish or where you'd like to go using words such as college, car, Paris, Fashion Designer, etc.
2. Look through magazines or search the Internet to find words or pictures that match your words in step 1.
3. Cut the pictures or words and attach them to the poster board with glue sticks or tape.
4. Hang or place the poster board where you can see it daily.

Remember that if you can see it, you can be it! So write it down, and then live it out!

Point to Ponder
Why is it important to make a dream board?

_____

_____

3. Turn Dreams into Reality

Dreaming is just the beginning; it's time to turn those dreams into concrete goals and take action. Remember, small steps lead to significant achievements. Prepare to set your goals and embark on your journey to your dreams!

A goal is simply a target or aim. For example, when I was in high school, one of my goals was to graduate from high school, which I did. I have had several goals in my lifetime, and you will, too. Some of your goals will be short-term goals that may take days, weeks, or months to accomplish. Getting a part-time job is a short-term goal. Other goals will be long-term ones that may take over a year, like purchasing a home.

Let's look at two more examples. Let's say your dream is to become a successful author. Your vision board may include images of books, inspirational quotes from famous authors, and a picture of a cozy writing space. Your goals could be to write a certain number of pages or chapters each week, attend writing workshops, and submit your work to publishers or writing contests.

Or your dream is to become a scientist working on groundbreaking discoveries. Your vision board could feature images of scientists in labs, research articles, and scientific quotes. Your goals may include studying science-related subjects, participating in science fairs, and seeking mentorship from professionals in the field.

Accomplishing a goal requires time and effort but is ultimately worth it. There are several steps to help you achieve a goal.

❖ Break down your dreams into smaller, actionable goals. Make them specific, measurable, achievable, relevant, and time-bound (SMART).

❖ Create an action plan. Outline the steps you need to take to achieve each goal and set deadlines for yourself.

❖ Take consistent action. Commit to taking small daily steps that bring you closer to your goals. Celebrate your progress, and don't be afraid to adjust your plans if needed. Here are a few examples:

As you go through these steps, you must have a positive outlook. Expect success! Persevere. Do not ever give up!

You will probably get discouraged or tired when you are trying to reach your goal; that is normal.

It's like when I ran track in high school. I did several things to win: I prepared physically and mentally, stayed in the right lane, jumped over hurdles, remained focused on the prize at the end, ran as if my life depended on it, and crossed the finish line. You can do it, so get to it!

Dream big, create a vision board, set goals, act, overcome obstacles, and celebrate success. That's the winning formula for turning your dreams into reality. Will you embrace the power of possibility? Will you visualize your dreams and set your goals to achieve them? I trust you will.

Remember, the journey may have twists and turns, but perseverance and determination can make your dreams come true. So, go out there, believe in yourself, and make it happen because you can do extraordinary things!

Point to Ponder
What is the first thing you must do to make your dream a reality?

_____

_____

Affirmation
Today, I will take the limits off my dreams and dream big!

Dream It

DIPLOMA

Making A Difference

FAMILY

travel

HELPING OTHERS

HAPPY

I LOVE ME

then DO IT

Reflect and Write

1. What would you do if you could accomplish your biggest, wildest dream without worrying about money?

_____

_____

_____

_____

_____

_____

_____

2. Write down one goal you'd like to reach in six months, a year, and five years.

a. In six months, I'd like to accomplish the following:

_____

_____

_____

_____

_____

_____

b. In one year, I'd like to accomplish the following:

_____

_____

_____

_____

_____

c. In five years, I'd like to accomplish the following:

_____

_____

_____

_____

_____

3. Why is it important to set goals?

_____

_____

_____

_____

_____

_____

_____

4. Is it better to set lower goals than to risk failure by establishing higher ones? Why or why not?

_____

_____

_____

_____

_____

_____

5. Have you taken the risk of failure to achieve a goal? What happened? Are you glad you took that risk?

_____

_____

_____

_____

_____

_____

_____

_____

6. What is the difference between failing and *being* a failure?

_____

_____

_____

_____

_____

_____

_____

_____

_____

_____

_____

I MIND MY OWN BUSINESS

GREAT GIRLS BECOME GREAT WOMEN

C.E.O

A GIRL'S GUIDE TO BEING GREAT

SCENARIO FOR PURSUING YOUR DREAMS

Sophia, Valerie, Rosita, and India were a tight-knit group of teenage girls with big dreams. They had each faced setbacks along the way, but they were determined not to let anything hold them back.

Sophia, the aspiring artist, had been rejected from an art school she had set her heart on. Despite the disappointment, she refused to let it crush her spirits. Instead, she decided to create her own path. With her friends' unwavering support and encouragement, Sophia started showcasing her artwork in local galleries and online platforms. She poured her heart and soul into her creations and soon gained recognition and a growing fan base. Sophia's resilience and talent showed that rejection didn't define her.

Valerie, the ambitious musician, had faced numerous rejections from record labels. But she believed in her music and refused to let setbacks discourage her. Determined to make her mark, Valeria took matters into her own hands. Valerie started performing at small venues, pouring her heart into every note she sang. She took to social media, sharing her songs with the world. Her powerful voice and captivating performances caught the attention of music lovers far and wide. Slowly but surely, Valerie's talent began to make waves in the industry, eventually leading to a record deal that fulfilled her dreams.

Rosita, the aspiring scientist, had experienced setbacks in her academic journey. She struggled with some subjects, and her grades could have been better. However, she possessed an unyielding passion for discovery and a drive to succeed. Rosita refused to let her setbacks define her intelligence or potential. She sought help from her teachers, formed study groups with her friends, and dedicated extra hours to her studies. Rosita mastered complex concepts Through sheer determination, surpassed her expectations, and achieved remarkable academic progress. Her hard work paid off when she received a scholarship to pursue her scientific dreams at a prestigious university, proving that setbacks were merely steppingstones to success.

India, the budding entrepreneur, faced multiple setbacks in her business ventures. Some of her ideas failed to take off, and others didn't yield the expected results. However, India possessed an unwavering entrepreneurial spirit and an unquenchable thirst for success. She refused to let setbacks dampen her passion and drive. Instead, she embraced failures as learning opportunities, allowing them to shape her entrepreneurial journey. India adjusted her strategies, sought guidance from mentors, and persisted with a positive mindset. Her steadfast determination and resilience eventually paid off as she successfully launched a startup that gained recognition and attracted investors. India proved that setbacks were merely detours, not dead ends.

Throughout their journeys, Sophia, Valerie, Rosita, and India face setbacks, but they never let those setbacks define them. Their shared experiences brought them closer together, forging an unbreakable bond of support, encouragement, and empowerment.

They celebrated each other's successes, constantly reminding them that their detours would not define them. Together, they proved that pursuing dreams would require resilience, determination, and a never-give-up attitude.

_____

_____

_____

_____

_____

_____

_____

_____

_____

_____

_____

_____

_____

_____

_____

_____

_____

_____

_____

_____

DO IT AFRAID

A Girl's Guide to Being Great

I DARE YOU

Dare to dream ~
The dream that births opportunities.
The dream that leaves legacies
Where you're the essence of royalty;
Then, wake up and make it a reality.

Dare to soar ~
Soar higher and faster than you have before
With a wind force that no one can ignore.
Above pettiness and the world's affairs
– A place where you know that someone cares.

Dare to be different ~
Different from the models in the magazines
Where their image is, many times, borderline obscene.
Recognize that it's not your genes but your mentality,
That makes you a mighty queen.

Dare to make choices ~
Choices that inspire, not kill.
Choices that give life and heal.
Choices that build and don't destroy.
Choices that yield unspeakable joy.

Don't allow yourself to be misled.
And choke on the lies you've been fed.
Don't be blurred by the tears that you have shed -
There are much brighter days ahead.

(Continued on next page)

When doubt and fear come your way,
Do not sway or dismay.
When people's attacks try to throw you off track
Remember, mercy and grace have got your back.

So, what is the dream that's been burning in you?
What is the thing that's been purposed for you?
What is the one thing someone said you can't do?
That might be the dream you make come true.

So, dream! Soar! Be different!
Don't be dismayed by the days you've spent.
Settling for second and indecision.
Make your dream come to fruition.

Some of the most incredible things you've heard or seen.
Have been done by people who've dared to dream!

So, go ahead. Dream! Push! Pursue!
Show me the power of what a made-up mind can do.
And see for yourself that your dream can come true.
I dare you to dream. I double-dog dare you.

7

LEADING WITH PURPOSE

"If your actions inspire others to dream more, learn more,
do more and become more, you are a leader."
~John Quincy Adams (1767 - 1848)
Sixth President of the United States

Get ready to step into the spotlight and discover your leadership potential. Did you know you can become a leader at your age and positively impact the world?

Leadership isn't just about a fancy title or being in charge; it's about guiding others, making a difference, and setting an example. So, let's dive in and unleash the leader within you!

What exactly is leadership? Leadership isn't limited to a specific role or position—it's a mindset and a way of living. It's about using your strengths, passions, and values to inspire and empower others. A true leader leads with integrity, authenticity, and compassion.

It's time to embrace your unique leadership style and make a difference in your unique way.

Point to Ponder
What does lead to lead with integrity?

_____

_____

_____

_____

1. Lead by Example

One of the most powerful ways to lead is by setting a positive example for others. Remember, actions speak louder than words.

I know you've seen plenty of people who offer advice, but they do the opposite of what they tell others to do. Here's an example:

Tina, a charming girl, was the hall monitor in school. She was always at her job; you could never get by Tina without your hall pass. Tina was tough and did not let anybody bend the rules! If Tina caught you outside of your classroom without a hall pass, she would write you up for detention, no matter if you were her brother, sister, or friend! Tina was just that serious about her job.

One day, Tina was outside her class without a hall pass. The principal put her in detention for not following the school's rules. You can bet your $5 that the ENTIRE school found out because news travels fast in a high school.

Tina felt ashamed and embarrassed that she had to go to detention, which is understandable because she always ensured others followed the rules and did not follow them herself. When the student body found out, they constantly reminded Tina that she could not tell them what to do because she was not doing what she was enforcing. Tina needed to lead by example, but she didn't, so her followers doubted her leadership abilities.

From that day on, Tina had to earn her respect back from her peers because they were not hearing anything she said. You might say, "Everybody makes mistakes," but consequences follow every mistake. Sometimes, it is difficult to regain trust once it's lost. That is why leading by example from the beginning is so important.

Here are some ways to do this:

- ❖ Embrace kindness and respect in your interactions with others. Also, please treat everyone with dignity, regardless of their background or differences.

- ❖ Demonstrate a strong work ethic and dedication in your pursuits. Whether in academics, personal projects, or extracurricular activities, show others your commitment, integrity, and determination.

- ❖ Take responsibility for your actions and admit when you make mistakes. Show humility and a willingness to learn from those experiences.

Point to Ponder
How do you feel about someone who does not lead by example?

_____

_____

2. Leaders Follow Other Leaders
True leaders understand that leadership is about learning from other leaders. Iron sharpens iron, so seek out mentors, role models, and inspiring figures who can guide and inspire you.

Here's how to follow other leaders:

Explore organizations promoting young girls' leadership development, such as Girls Who Code, the National Student Leadership Conference, the United Nations Foundation's Girl Up, She's the First, and Teen Vogue's "21 Under 21, " showcasing teen leadership's power which empowers girls to become leaders and changemakers.

Don't underestimate your leadership ability because young girls can be phenomenal leaders! There are countless examples of those who have become successful and made a difference simultaneously, like Poet and Activist Amanda Gorman and American Professional Tennis Player Cori Dionne "Coco" Gauff. I've listed others at the end of this book to inspire you.

Also, connect with leaders within your community, school, or extracurricular activities. Observe their leadership styles and learn from their experiences.

Point to Ponder
Why should leaders follow other leaders?

_____

_____

3. You Can Be a Great Leader
Do you want to make a difference in the lives around you? Do people come to you for advice? If so, you might already be a leader. Guess what. Even if you are shy, you can still lead others. Leadership skills are teachable; you can learn them.

There are many opportunities to develop leadership skills in school, college, and the community. For example, you can join clubs and organizations such as the Debate Club, Future Business Leaders of America (FBLA), Student Council, and others in your school. You can also watch others as they lead or take an active leadership role, such as becoming the secretary or president of a club.

In college, Phi Beta Lambda is a great leadership organization where you can gain business skills, communication skills, and many other skills that can make you a better leader. Also, it gives you many opportunities to speak in front of an audience and participate in various competitions locally and across the state.

In the community, you can volunteer at various organizations, such as Habitat for Humanity, the Boys and Girls Club, and many others. If there's not an organization in which you are interested in being a part, start your organization or business. Many successful people became who they are today because they had an idea or saw a need and decided to start a company. You might be surprised, but some of them were about your age!

To develop your leadership skills, associate with people who are leaders. Improve your speaking and communication skills through classes at your school or community. An excellent organization that helps you do this is Toastmasters International. Also, let your teachers know you desire to become a leader and ask them to help you.

Becoming a leader requires hard work, sacrifice, dedication, continuous learning, integrity, and more. So why should you lead others? What's in it for you?

When you become a leader, you positively influence people and improve situations. In addition, leaders guide and inspire others. Did you know you can make a good living using your leadership skills in business?

> As a young lady, you owe it to others to be the best you can be and to use your leadership skills to benefit others.

I encourage you to inspire, empower, and lead those around you. Step into your leadership role with confidence, authenticity, and a commitment to making a difference. The world needs your leadership, and you are capable of extraordinary things. Just like I am empowering you through the words of this book, you can empower others.

Point to Ponder
What can you do to increase your leadership skills now?

_____

_____

Affirmation
I declare that I will use my leadership skills to inspire others.

Reflect and Write

1. Using the acronym LEADER, list a characteristic leaders should possess.

L – _____

E – _____

A – _____

D – _____

E – _____

R – _____

2. Do you think you can be a great leader? Why or why not?

_____

_____

_____

_____

3. What advice would you give someone having trouble being a positive role model for others?

_____

_____

_____

_____

_____

_____

4. What factors should you consider when taking a leadership role?

_____

_____

_____

_____

_____

5. What organizations can you join at school or in the community to develop your leadership skills?

_____

_____

_____

_____

_____

6. In what areas are you leading by example at home or among friends?

_____

_____

_____

_____

_____

_____

Bonus Scenario for Leading with Purpose

In the small town of Beaver Creek, four teenage girls named Lisa, Chasity, Pam, and Brianna decided to shake things up in their community. They were tired of sitting around and waiting for someone else to make a difference, so they banded together to create positive change.

Lisa, a natural-born leader, took charge and suggested they start a community garden. She believed it would beautify the town and promote healthier eating habits. The girls loved the idea and immediately got to work. They convinced the local government to provide them with a vacant lot, and with their sheer determination, they transformed it into a vibrant garden full of colorful flowers and delicious vegetables.

Chasity, the tech-savvy girl of the group, came up with the idea of creating a website and social media pages to promote their community garden. She snapped terrific pictures of their progress and shared them online. Soon, the entire town was buzzing with excitement, and people from all walks of life began to take an interest in their initiative.

With her kind heart and love for helping others, Pam proposed that they donate a portion of the garden's harvest to local food banks. She knew many families were in need, and this small gesture could make a big difference. The girls agreed wholeheartedly and started organizing weekly donations. The joy they saw on the faces of those receiving the fresh produce motivated them even further.

Brianna, the creative soul, suggested organizing events at the garden to engage the community. They hosted workshops on gardening, cooking, and sustainable living. Families gathered to learn new skills and bond over shared experiences. These events brought the town together and created a sense of unity that was missing before.

As time passed, their garden flourished, their online presence grew, and their impact on the community was undeniable. Lisa, Chasity, Pam, and Brianna had proven that age was just a number for leading with purpose. They showed their town that anyone, regardless of age, could make a difference and create positive change.

Their inspiring story spread far beyond Beaver Creek, and other communities soon took note. Teenagers nationwide started their initiatives, leading with purpose and making a lasting impact in their neighborhoods.

And so, the four girls continued their journey, empowering others and leaving a legacy of leadership and community spirit. They showed the world that when young people come together with passion and purpose, there is no limit to what they can achieve.

What are your thoughts about this scenario?

_____

_____

_____

_____

_____

_____

_____

_____

_____

THE PARADOXICAL COMMANDMENTS
By Kent M. Keith
Printed with permission.

1. People are illogical, unreasonable, and self-centered. Love them anyway.
2. If you do good, people will accuse you of selfish ulterior motives. Do good anyway.
3. If you are successful, you will win false friends and true enemies. Succeed anyway.
4. The good you do today will be forgotten tomorrow. Do good anyway.
5. Honesty and frankness make you vulnerable. Be honest and frank anyway.
6. The biggest men and women with the biggest ideas can be shot down by the smallest men and women with the smallest minds. Think big anyway.
7. People favor underdogs but follow only top dogs. Fight for a few underdogs anyway.
8. What you spend years building may be destroyed overnight. Build anyway.
9. People really need help but may attack you if you do help them. Help people anyway.
10. Give the world your best, and you'll get kicked in the teeth. Give the world the best you have anyway.

I have the POWER to Change the WORLD

A GIRL'S GUIDE TO BEING GREAT

8

Handling Media Mania

*"We perceive and are affected by changes to
subtle to be described."*
~Henry David Thoreau (1817 – 1862)
American author, poet, and philosopher

Do you think someone you don't know personally can influence you to behave in a certain way? You are affected by the media more than you think. Believe it or not, many of your beliefs and actions result from what you've seen or heard, and often, you do not realize it because the messages are so subtle. Once you *agree* to the idea, you *accept* it as the norm, *approve* it as accurate, and sometimes *act* on it, knowingly or unknowingly.

In this chapter, we peel back the layers and expose the power of media, especially social media, on our lives. Media is everywhere, bombarding us with messages, images, and stories that shape our perceptions. We also define what media and social media are all about and uncover their subtle and sometimes dangerous influence on teen girls.

When discussing media, we talk about how information and entertainment reach us. It includes everything from TV shows, movies, music, magazines, newspapers, and the ever-present social media platforms. Media is like a giant spotlight, focusing on specific ideas, trends, and beauty standards. But here's the thing: the media doesn't always reflect reality, nor is it always helpful.

Let's focus on social media, hashtags, likes, and viral videos. It's where we share our lives, connect with friends, and discover new trends. But beneath the shiny surface, social media can influence us negatively.

Social media bombards us with carefully curated feeds, flawless selfies, and seemingly perfect lives. It's easy to get caught up in the comparison game, thinking we don't measure up.

Social media bombards us with carefully curated feeds, flawless selfies, and seemingly perfect lives. It's easy to get caught up in the comparison game, thinking we don't measure up.

But here's the truth: those picture-perfect posts only show one side of the story. They don't capture the messy, real moments.

Remember, unlike social media, real life isn't filtered, cropped, or photoshopped. Let's explore more.

Point to Ponder
What form of media influences you the most? Why?

_____

_____

1. What You Listen to Matters

Music

When you listen to the radio, you are most likely being influenced by the songs or messages you hear, one way or another.

Meet Kaitlyn. Kaitlyn is a sophomore in high school who said, "It doesn't matter if a boy calls a girl the "B" word in a song because I know that he isn't talking to me." Most of the girls in that class agreed and said that it was not harmful to listen to songs where the singers called them the "B" word because they didn't write the songs for them. But ladies, that's a problem.

Kaitlyn thought that the words were not harmful (she agreed with them) and began *accepting* them as just part of the song or the way boys talked about girls. Then, she *approved* and *acted* on them by listening, singing, and dancing to the song's words. She was unaware that the words she sang became a part of her identity.

> Music should be a positive form of entertainment that makes you dance or feel good. It should uplift your spirit and bring joy to your life. However, when songs refer to you negatively, then they should have no place in your life.

Just think. If every girl would stop listening to songs from both male and female artists that disrespect them, we would likely see an increase in self-esteem among girls.

Music should be a positive form of entertainment that makes you feel good. It should uplift your spirit and bring joy. However, when songs are filled with profanity and refer to you negatively, they should have no place in your life.

Point to Ponder
Do you agree with Kaitlyn? Why or why not?

_____

_____

_____

2. What You See Matters

Magazine Ads

Let's talk about magazine ads, you know, the ones—the flawless models, the perfect bodies, and the airbrushed perfection. If you flip through a magazine designed for teen girls or women, you will see that many of them feature beauty products and the latest fashion trends to make you feel that she should look a certain way. No wonder some girls think they're not enough! But guess what? Those ads consist of carefully crafted illusions. They're not real. Please don't let them make you feel inadequate or unattractive.

Embrace your uniqueness, celebrate your individuality, and know you are enough just as you are. Don't let those ads fool you into thinking otherwise. You're beautiful inside and out; no glossy page can define your worth.

Television

Watching television can be entertaining and educational, but do you realize how much television programs influence you?

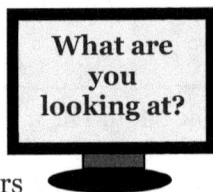

What are you looking at?

Some programs are harmless, but others are the opposite. For example, shows that glamorize people fighting, being rebellious, using profanity, and engaging in risky behaviors are scripted for ratings.

For example, popular shows that follow the lives of "housewives" give the impression that verbally and physically fighting with other women is acceptable and expected, but this is far from the truth.

Also, programs that glamorize girls being mean towards other girls can lead you to believe that bullying and disrespecting others is cool or the norm. It's not. Therefore, don't be a mean girl; be a "great" girl!

Reality television usually does not depict anyone's *real* life and not their ideal life, so do not use these shows as a standard of how you should behave or who you should be.

> Reality television usually does not depict anyone's *real* life and definitely not their ideal life, so do not use these shows as a standard of how you should behave or who you should be.

Social Media (YouTube, TikTok, Facebook, etc.)

Platforms like YouTube, Instagram, TikTok, and Facebook impact you.

One major downside is the pressure to be perfect. Teenage girls often stumble upon influencers who seem to have it all together. They see flawless faces, perfect bodies, and fabulous lifestyles. And what happens? It often makes them feel like they need to be measuring up.

They start comparing themselves and feeling self-conscious about their appearance and achievements. It's like a constant reminder that they're not good enough. For instance, seeing those Insta models with chiseled abs and fancy vacations might make a girl question her body and feel insecure about her beach pics.

Then there's the issue of cyberbullying. Social media can sometimes be a breeding ground for mean comments, hate messages, and online harassment. Teenage girls can find themselves on the receiving end of hurtful words and targeted attacks. Imagine a girl posting a video expressing her opinions, only to face a barrage of nasty comments attacking her intelligence or appearance. It's not just hurtful—it can seriously mess with her self-esteem and mental well-being.

Let's remember the FOMO (Fear of Missing Out) factor. Social media bombards girls with images of parties, outings, and gatherings. They see their peers having what seems like the time of their lives, while they might feel left out at home. It can make them feel lonely, inadequate, and as though they are missing out on all the fun. Think about a girl scrolling through TikTok, seeing her friends dancing together at a party, and feeling sad because no one invited her. It's a tough pill to swallow.

Point to Ponder
What effect does watching reality TV shows and social media platforms (YouTube, TikTok, etc.) have on you?

_____

_____

<u>Music Videos</u>

Making and watching videos is still a favorite pastime among some teenagers. However, many of these videos need to send the right messages.

Meet Christina. Christina was a girl in the 10th grade who enjoyed watching music videos. When asked what she wanted to do for a living when she finished school, Christina said, "I want to star in a music video." Although surprised initially, I realized Christina probably viewed this as a way to make quick money or to be popular. Plus, she saw nothing wrong with wearing hardly any clothes and dancing to music as people cheered her on with drinks, so this was her career aspiration.

Sadly, many of these videos, produced primarily by men, stereotype girls. As a result, when girls watch these videos, they begin to dress in tight, short, or revealing clothes, thinking that it is acceptable to behave this way. Regrettably, girls often become labeled, targeted, and not taken seriously. These actions can lead to low self-esteem, depression, and a life full of heartache. Please decide that this will not be you. Aspire to be more than that.

Commercials

> ...When girls watch these videos, many of them begin to dress in very tight, short, or revealing clothes, thinking that it is acceptable to behave this way. Regrettably, they oftentimes become labeled, targeted, and not taken seriously.

Sometimes, the message used in advertising needs to be more truthful. Some ads can make you feel you are not "good enough" when you are more than enough.

Numerous commercials about exercising and dieting are frequently on television. Most models in these ads are slim and "beautiful," as defined by society. As a result, these ads convey that a girl should look a certain way if she wants to fit in or for others to like her.

Sadly, many girls compare themselves to those models. When they don't measure up, they sometimes engage in unhealthy or unnecessary behaviors, such as dieting or starving to lose weight. They might also start acting out and develop low self-esteem.

Don't accept the lie that you must fit into someone's idea of what makes someone pretty. The truth is that you are breathtakingly beautiful!

> Don't accept the lie that you must fit into someone's idea of what makes someone pretty. The truth is that you are breathtakingly beautiful!

But what's more important than your appearance is that you are healthy. You want to be your *best* and be physically fit for your body type. So, take care of yourself by exercising, eating a nutritious diet, getting proper rest, thinking positive thoughts, and having the right people in your life.

Remember, you don't need to change your appearance for someone else's approval. You are beautiful inside and out, just like you are.

And you do not have to believe or respond to what you see or hear in the media. When you see commercials, analyze them and ask yourself: What message is this sending me? Who is the source of this message, and what is in it for them?

Point to Ponder
Why is it important to understand the underlying messages in advertisements regarding women?

_____

_____

3. What You Say and Show Matters

The Internet and Social Media

The Internet, or the "information highway," puts information at a person's fingertip 24/7.

Social media can be a fun way to connect with others. Many teenagers use social media like Facebook, Twitter, and

Instagram, among others, to communicate. Some use YouTube to make videos and upload them to gain followers.

> Remember that once a picture or video is posted on the Internet or sent in a text, you have no control over what happens to it. You can't simply hit delete to make it go away.

But a big problem with social media is that some use it in a potentially harmful way: to bully other girls, to tell their business, to let people know if they are in a relationship, to share where they are, and to post pictures of themselves. Some of these actions, while innocent, can have dangerous consequences.

For instance, some unsuspecting girls use poor judgment and give their personal information to someone who is not who they seem. And countless tragic stories exist of girls who sent inappropriate pictures to someone they liked. But then that person threatens to share their photos with classmates and on the world wide web if they don't send more.

Remember that once a picture or video is posted on the Internet or sent in a text, you have no control over what happens to it. You can't simply hit delete to make it go away. They can go viral in minutes, and deleting them won't make them disappear.

So take it from me as someone with a degree in Cybercrime and Criminal Justice: if you do not want something shared with the world, do not text, write, or post it on social media! I realize it's the norm for this society, but it's much better to be safe than sorry.

Also, when you use social media, imagine how you would feel if your mother, grandmother, youth leader, pastor, teacher, child, or future boss got a hold of your pictures and posts. Would you be embarrassed? Would they be disappointed?

Therefore, don't just think about the moment you take or post pictures. Consider who might see them years from now and how you might feel about them later. You might view things differently than you do now when you are older. Don't let your words or pictures come back to haunt you.

> When you take or post pictures, think about who might see those years from now and how you might feel about them later.

3. Weigh the Rewards and Risks

Media and social media can be helpful and harmful, impacting your life negatively and positively.

Here are some common challenges:

❖ **Unrealistic Beauty Standards:** Media often portrays narrow and idealistic beauty ideals, leading to body image issues, low self-esteem, and comparison among teen girls. Constantly exposing edited and curated images can create a distorted perception of what is attractive.

❖ **Cyberbullying and Online Harassment**: Social media platforms can become breeding grounds for cyberbullying, harassment, and negative comments. You may experience verbal attacks, rumors, exclusion, or threats, harming your mental health and well-being.

❖ **Social Comparison and FOMO:** Social media can amplify feelings of social comparison and the fear of missing out (FOMO). Seeing others' highlight reels, experiences, and social activities can make you feel inadequate or left out, contributing to loneliness, anxiety, and depression.

❖ **Privacy and Online Safety:** Maintaining privacy and online safety can significantly concern teen girls. Sharing personal information, images, or location details can put you at risk of online predators, identity theft, or exploitation. Additionally, the permanence of online content can have long-term consequences.

❖ **Not Everything's True**: Sometimes, the media can be misleading or biased. Don't take everything at face value. Fact-checking and digging deeper are essential to get the full story so you don't believe lies.

❖ **Influence of Influencers and Advertising:** Teen girls frequently become targets of influencers and celebrities who promote products, services, or lifestyles. This influencer culture can lead to materialism, peer pressure, and an emphasis on external validation, affecting your self-perception and spending habits.

❖ **Screen Time Balance**: Spending too much time on social media can impact our mental health and take away from real-life experiences. Finding a healthy balance and taking breaks to engage in other activities you enjoy is essential.

❖ **Mental Health Impact:** Excessive use of social media can contribute to increased anxiety, depression, and feelings of social isolation.

In contrast, here are some upsides of the media:

❖ **Informative and Fun:** Media is a great way to get information and stay current on what's happening worldwide. Plus, it offers tons of entertainment like movies, shows, music, and books that we all love!

❖ **Representation Matters:** Media shows people from different backgrounds and cultures, helping us feel represented and showing us that we can achieve anything if we make up our minds.

❖ **Empowering Voices:** Media gives you a voice to speak up about issues you care about. It can be a powerful tool to raise awareness, fight for causes you believe in, and make a positive change.

❖ **Connecting with Friends**: Social media lets you stay associated with friends, no matter where they are. It's fun to share moments, chat, and support each other.

❖ **Finding Support:** Social media communities can be a great source of support when going through tough times. You can find like-minded people, join groups, and feel less alone.

❖ **Express Yourself:** Social media gives you a platform to express your creativity, showcase your talents, and share your thoughts and opinions.

Remember, media and social media can be excellent communication methods and entertainment sources, but using them wisely is crucial. Stay informed, be critical, be kind to yourself and others, and don't forget to enjoy the real world too!

Point to Ponder
Will you use social media or texts to say hurtful or untrue things about someone? Why or why not?

_____

_____

_____

Affirmation
I will consider what the media is saying to me. If it is untrue or harmful, I will not give it my time or attention.

I Don't Blend In I Stand Out

Reflect and Write

1. Have you heard the words to a song that made you feel uncomfortable, but you listened to it song anyway? Why?

_____

_____

_____

_____

_____

_____

_____

_____

2. How can you use social media to uplift and inspire girls?

_____

_____

_____

_____

_____

_____

_____

_____

_____

_____

3. Write a short letter to a television show producer who does not positively characterize women. Explain to the producer how the show affects you, why it is offensive, or what changes they could make to show women in a more positive light. You can also write a letter to a singer about a song you find offensive to women.

_____

_____

_____

_____

_____

_____

_____

_____

_____

_____

_____

_____

_____

_____

_____

_____

_____

_____

4. Image is everything. Do you have inappropriate pictures of you on Facebook or other social media? "Inappropriate" means your clothes are too tight, short, or revealing. What do your clothes and your poses suggest to others? If you are unsure, ask an adult who you trust. If your pictures are questionable, will you remove them? Why or why not?

_____

_____

_____

_____

_____

_____

_____

_____

_____

_____

_____

_____

_____

_____

_____

MARCH TO THE BEAT OF MY OWN DRUM

A Girl's Guide to Being Great

Bonus Scenario for Taking Control of Media Mania

Meet Gail, Yolanda, Anita, and Norma. These girls were tired of how the media portrayed them and their fellow girls. They felt the media always focused on the same old stereotypes and never showcased their true potential. So, they decided to take matters into their own hands and take control of the media.

Gail, the tech-savvy girl, came up with a brilliant idea. She suggested they start their own YouTube channel. They could create videos celebrating girls' diverse talents and interests in their town. Gail believed that by showcasing real girls doing extraordinary things, they could inspire others and break those tired stereotypes.

Yolanda, the fearless and charismatic one, loved the idea. She suggested they start with a video series called "Girls Unleashed," where they would feature interviews with girls excelling in various fields. They could interview star athletes, aspiring scientists, budding entrepreneurs, and even talented artists. Yolanda believed that sharing these stories could help shift the narrative and show the world that girls are capable of anything.

Anita, the creative mind, thought of adding a touch of humor and satire to their content. She suggested they create parody videos, mocking the unrealistic beauty standards set by the media. They could create hilarious skits, like "Makeup Mishaps," where they deliberately overdid their makeup to show how silly it can get. Anita believed laughter was a powerful tool to challenge societal norms and help girls embrace natural beauty.

Norma, the passionate activist, wanted to address social issues. She suggested they create powerful short documentaries on body positivity, gender equality, and mental health awareness. Norma believed that by shedding light on these critical issues, they could ignite conversations and drive positive change in their community.

Excited and enthusiastic, the four girls set their plan in motion. They started filming videos, editing like pros, and unleashing their creativity. They created a YouTube channel called "GYN (Girls You Need) Media" and shared their first video, "Meet the Unstoppable Girls of Oakville."

To their surprise, their videos started gaining traction quickly. Girls from their towns and beyond began sharing their stories and talents. Viewers loved the humor, the inspiring interviews, and the thought-provoking documentaries. The media even took notice, and soon enough, local news outlets featured stories about these extraordinary girls who were making a difference.

Gail, Yolanda, Anita, and Norma realized they had started a movement as their channel grew. They inspired other girls to take control of their narratives, creating content and challenging social norms. Together, they formed a supportive community of like-minded individuals determined to change the media landscape for good.

Ultimately, Gail, Yolanda, Anita, and Norma proved that teenage girls could reclaim the media. They showed that by amplifying authentic voices and embracing diversity, they could shape a media that truly represented them and empowered other girls. Their journey taught them that with passion, creativity, and a supportive team, they could make a lasting impact and create a world where girls could shine unapologetically.

And so, the four girls continued their media transformation, one video at a time, inspiring countless others to join their cause.

What are your thoughts about this scenario?

_____

_____

_____

_____

_____

_____

_____

_____

_____

_____

_____

_____

_____

_____

_____

_____

_____

_____

_____

*Optional   Activities   for   Extended   Learning

1. Look through magazines and analyze the ads. What are they selling? Who is the product for? What images are they using to sell the products? What message do you get from the ad?

_____

_____

_____

_____

_____

_____

_____

2. Listen closely to song lyrics and examine the message behind the songs. To whom are they written, and why? How do you feel when you listen to them? Why do you think so?

_____

_____

_____

_____

_____

_____

_____

_____

_____

_____

THE INFLUENCE OF THE MEDIA

When I look in magazines, many of the ads I see
Tell me how I am is not how I "should" be.
There are ads with beauty products to hide my blemishes:
Make-up, bronzers, lipsticks – the list seems endless:

Diet pills and exercise bikes to help me lose weight,
5" heels with studs or spikes to wear on a date;
Teeth whitener, skin brightener, and color for my hair.
Sheer shirts and mini-skirts – wear them if I dare.

When I watch television, many women I see
Are in bad relationships for the whole world to see;
Many of them are desperate, while others curse and fight;
Some have bad morals, but others get it right.

When I look on Facebook, some of what I see.
Bring sadness and embarrassment to the woman in me:
Some people leave little to the imagination
And give personal information without hesitation.

When I listen to certain music, the words are so disgraceful.
I wonder why people buy music so distasteful:
Words that promote violence and stereotypes;
Drugs, profanity, drama, and hype;
Words that glorify violence without any shame,
And demean women's worth in exchange for fame.

So, I will not listen to music or read articles in magazines.
Nor watch TV programs if the message is not clean.
I will not let the media dictate how I feel.
But instead, dissect the messages and decipher what is real.

It's my time to shine

A Girl's Guide to Being Great

9

Managing Relationships & Dating

"Relationships should be a source of joy and growth, not a place where you compromise your worth."
- Arianna Huffington

Relationships and dating come with their share of emotions, with highs, lows, and everything in between.

Sometimes, you meet a friend, and it's an instant connection – you click. Other moments will make your heart skip a beat— those exciting highs when you connect with someone who gets you and makes you feel warm and fuzzy. It's like finding your favorite song on repeat, with butterflies fluttering in your stomach.

But don't get too excited too soon because some relationships involve drama and trauma. You might face misunderstandings, disagreements, or even heartbreak. It's like a low blow to the gut. But guess what? These lows are an opportunity for growth and learning. They teach you about communication, compromise, and setting boundaries. Remember, it's not always a bed of roses, but your challenges can make your connection more meaningful.

Communication is key. Talk openly, honestly, and kindly with your partner. Share your feelings, listen actively, and work together to find solutions. Remember, you are a team, so your relationship should not be one-sided.

But there is also the art of balance. Your relationship shouldn't consume you or become a priority over your personal life. Keep pursuing your goals, spending time with friends, and indulging in your hobbies. It's all about finding that sweet spot where you can be your fabulous self while being part of a relationship that *adds* value to your life and does not *become* your life.

> Boundaries are like the invisible force that protects your emotional well-being. Saying " No " is okay if something feels wrong or you need space. Respect your own boundaries, and make sure your partner does too.

And let's remember the importance of boundaries. Boundaries are like the invisible force that protects your emotional well-being. Saying " No " is okay if something feels wrong or you need space. Respect your limits, and make sure your partner does too.

Remember, a healthy relationship involves mutual respect, trust, and consent.

Relating with someone emotionally or intimately allows you to learn about yourself, your preferences, and how you relate to others. Through dating, you gain insights into your needs, wants, and values and how to communicate and negotiate with a romantic partner. These experiences contribute to your growth and help shape your understanding of healthy relationships.

Point to Ponder
List one or two positive aspects of dating.

_____

_____

1. Dating Presents Many Complex Challenges

Dating can be a joyful experience for teenage girls. It's when you get to know someone special, share your feelings and create meaningful connections. However, along with happiness, dating can also bring about specific challenges.

Here are a few:

❖ **Peer pressure** Teenagers often face pressures to conform to specific dating rules or engage in behaviors that go against their principles.

❖ **Pressure for physical intimacy:** There can be societal pressure to become intimate before you are ready. So, set clear boundaries and make informed decisions about your comfort levels.

❖ **Online dating and cyberbullying:** With the rise of social media and online dating platforms, many girls may face online harassment, bullying, or encounters with potential predators.

❖ **Balancing dating with other responsibilities:** Teenagers often have multiple commitments, such as schoolwork, extracurricular activities, and family obligations. Juggling these responsibilities with dating can be challenging and lead to stress and a lack of balance.

❖ **Impact on self-esteem:** Relationships during the teenage years can significantly influence your self-esteem and self-worth. Negative experiences or rejection in dating can potentially impact your confidence and emotional well-being.

❖ **Dating violence:** Unfortunately, some teen girls may experience dating violence, including emotional, physical, or sexual abuse. Remember that love doesn't hurt. Get help to get out of that relationship immediately.

❖ **Understanding the "Girl Code":** The concept of a "girl code" varies among individuals and cultures, but it generally refers to a set of unwritten rules or guidelines that some women follow regarding dating, relationships, and friendships.

Here are some common aspects of the girl code:

  o **Offer support:** Girls often prioritize being honest and supportive to their friends in dating matters, including providing advice, listening to concerns, and being there for each other emotionally.

  o **Respect boundaries:** Respecting each other's boundaries is essential. It means not pursuing someone your friend is interested in, not dating an ex-partner without their consent, and not sharing intimate details about your friend's romantic life without their permission.

  o **Avoid betrayal**: Girls are not expected to date or get involved with a friend's ex-boyfriend or crush immediately after a breakup to avoid feelings of betrayal and to maintain the friendship.

  o **Communication:** Open and transparent communication is vital. Girls often encourage each other to talk openly about their feelings, expectations, and intentions with their partners.

    o **Lending a helping hand:** Friends expect to support each other through dating challenges. Examples include providing feedback on outfits, helping with makeup or hair, or assisting in preparing for dates.

Although these "Girl Code" guidelines are not universal, the most crucial aspect of any code, whether girl code or any other, silent or spoken, is mutual respect, trust, *and* open communication between friends.

Point to Ponder
List one or two challenges of dating.

_____

_____

2. Heartbreak Happens

Heartbreak is an experience that can vary from person to person. However, here are some strategies you may find helpful in coping with sorrow:

❖ **Allow yourself to feel:** It's normal to experience a wide range of emotions after a breakup, including sadness, anger, and confusion. Give yourself permission to acknowledge and experience these emotions fully. Allow yourself to cry and express your feelings.

❖ **Seek support**: Reach out to friends, family, or a support network to discuss your feelings. Sharing your emotions with trusted individuals can provide comfort and perspective. Sometimes, professional help from a therapist or counselor can also be beneficial.

❖ **Take care of yourself**: Prioritize self-care during this difficult time. Engage in activities that you enjoy and that promote your well-being, such as exercise, hobbies, spending time in nature, or relaxation techniques. Pay attention to your physical health by maintaining a balanced diet, getting enough sleep, and staying hydrated.

❖ **Give yourself time and space**: Healing takes time, so be patient. Avoid rushing into a new relationship to escape the pain. Take time to reflect on the relationship and learn from the experience. Giving yourself space to heal and regain your sense of self is crucial.

❖ **Avoid excessive self-blame:** It's common to feel responsible for the breakup or to dwell on what could have happened differently. However, remember that it takes two people to make the relationship work. Avoid blaming yourself excessively, and try to practice self-compassion.

Everyone's healing process is unique, and no one-size-fits-all approach exists. It's okay to seek professional help if you're struggling with heartbreak. Ultimately, with time, self-care, and support, most people find their way through the healing process and emerge stronger on the other side.

Point to Ponder
What is one way you will handle heartbreak?

_____

_____

_____

_____

3. The Sex Factor

Dating allows you to experience various aspects of intimacy, including emotional support, companionship, and physical affection. Naturally, the issue of sex will come up.

While you might feel like you're missing out if you don't give in, don't cave to the pressure of being sexually intimate. After all, do you really want to do something you aren't ready for to prove your love? Do you want to have lifelong regrets about giving such a personal part of yourself to someone who doesn't appreciate or demonstrate how exceptional you are?

Here's the deal: If someone cares about you, they will not ask you to do something against your beliefs.

But suppose *you're* the one who wants to become intimate? Weigh the risks of giving in to your desire.

Here are several factors to seriously consider before engaging in sexual behavior:

❖ **What are your values and beliefs**? How do your personal, cultural, or religious values shape your decision about sexual behavior?

❖ **Are you emotionally ready?** When you are intimate with someone, you become emotionally attached to them, and it isn't easy to move on like nothing happened. How do you handle it if they don't feel the same way? How do you feel when they have other partners?

❖ **Are you physically ready?** Do you understand reproductive health, and are you aware of and prepared for the potential risks associated with sexual behavior?

❖ **Do you understand relationship dynamics**? Engaging in sexual behavior can profoundly impact relationships. Consider prioritizing building solid emotional connections and developing healthy relationship dynamics first.

❖ **How will becoming sexually active or sending nude pictures affect your education and future goals?** Will you become distracted and lose focus? What happens if you become pregnant? What do you do if someone shares private photos or messages with others or puts them online for the world?

One important thing to remember is that relationships should never define your worth. You are unique, lovable, and complete on your own.

Whether you're single or in a relationship, your value remains unchanged. Embrace your individuality, pursue your passions, and let love and romance complement your journey rather than define it.

Point to Ponder
What should you consider before becoming intimate with someone?

_____

_____

Affirmation
I can establish balance and set healthy boundaries in my relationships.

Reflect and Write

1. Why is having a healthy balance important in relationships?

_____

_____

_____

_____

_____

_____

2. Why is creating boundaries important in relationships?

_____

_____

_____

_____

_____

3. List three reasons you should not send revealing or nude pictures to someone.

_____

_____

_____

_____

_____

_____

4. What should you consider before getting in or continuing a relationship with someone?

_____

_____

_____

_____

_____

_____

5. What would you do if someone asked you to engage in sexual activities before you were ready?

_____

_____

_____

_____

_____

4. What is your takeaway from this chapter?

_____

_____

_____

_____

_____

_____

_____

Bonus for Managing Relationships & Dating

Britney, Skye, and Shakena were three best friends, and they were all exploring the world of relationships and dating. They faced their fair share of challenges but were determined to navigate them together.

Britney had been dating Ethan for a while, and things were going great. However, they started having disagreements that left Britney feeling frustrated. Instead of letting these issues simmer, they decided to sit down and have an honest chat. They shared their concerns, listened to each other's perspectives, and found compromises that worked for both. Britney learned that open communication was vital to working through relationship challenges.

Skye, the thoughtful and reflective one, struggled with trust in her relationship with Liam. She often felt insecure and worried he might be interested in someone else. Skye decided to have a heart-to-heart conversation with Liam about her fears. He reassured her of his commitment and encouraged her to trust their connection. Skye discovered that building trust required vulnerability and ongoing communication, helping her feel more secure in their relationship.

Shakena, the adventurous and sporty girl, faced the challenge of different hobbies with her boyfriend, Jake. She loved playing basketball, while Jake was more into video games. Instead of letting this divide them, they explored each other's interests. Shakena joined Jake for gaming sessions, and he joined Shakena on the basketball court. Through this experience, they found common ground and grew to respect each other's passions.

As their relationships progressed, the girls also dealt with the challenge of personal boundaries. Britney realized the importance of alone time to recharge her energy but sometimes felt guilty about expressing this to Ethan. They had an open conversation and set boundaries that allowed them personal space while encouraging their connection. Britney understood that it was healthy to prioritize self-care in a relationship.

Skye faced the challenge of balancing her relationship with Liam and her friendships. She worried about neglecting her friends and losing their bond. Skye tried to maintain her friendships by organizing hangouts and keeping in touch regularly. She learned that balancing her romantic relationship and friendships was crucial for her happiness and well-being.

Shakena encountered a tough challenge when Jake had to move away due to his father's job. They decided to give long-distance a shot. It was challenging, but they communicated regularly through calls, video chats, and text messages. They found creative ways to stay connected, like watching movies simultaneously or playing online games together. Shakena discovered that trust and communication could help sustain a long-distance relationship despite the distance.

Throughout their journey, Britney, Skye, and Shakena learned that relationships and dating come with challenges, but they were determined to overcome them. With their friendship as a solid foundation, they supported and guided each other through the ups and downs. They embraced the lessons learned, and together, they grew stronger in their relationships and as individuals.

What are your thoughts about this scenario?

_____

_____

_____

_____

_____

_____

_____

_____

_____

_____

_____

_____

_____

_____

_____

_____

_____

_____

_____

_____

NO ONE CAN DEFINE OR UNDERMINE ME

A Girl's Guide to Being Great

Hearts Entwined

In school and out, hearts collide,
With texts and smiles, feelings ride.
We navigate these crazy waves,
Through highs and lows, our bond engraves.

TikTok, stories, late-night calls,
Laughing at memes that hit the walls.
Late-night texts and selfies shared,
Emoji hearts show we care.

But sometimes drama creeps like fog,
Let's keep it real and cut through the smog.
Through ups and downs, we'll stick together.
Like matching shoes, we'll rock it, whether.

Through gossip storms or heartfelt chats,
Besties and crushes, we're more than that.
So let's embrace this crazy ride,
With trust and fun, we'll take it in stride,

Teen girls united, hearts entwined,
In friendships and love, we'll forever bind.

Nothing or no one will hold me back

A Girl's Guide to Being Great

10

Empowering Your Emotions

"Emotional well-being is not about being happy all the time. It's about embracing all your emotions, allowing yourself to feel them fully, and practicing self-compassion."
~Emma Watson, Actress, and UN Goodwill Ambassador

Life can sometimes feel like a roller coaster ride of emotions. From school stress to friendship dramas, taking care of your emotional well-being is crucial.

Emotions are like superheroes that can guide you through life's ups and downs. The key is embracing and empowering them and using them to your advantage.

First off, let's talk about the mighty power of positivity. Imagine waking up on a gloomy Monday morning, feeling a bit blah. Try shifting your mindset instead of allowing those negative vibes to consume you. Take a moment to reflect on what you're grateful for—a loving family, fantastic friends, or even a cozy bed. Focusing on the positive aspects will make you feel more energized and ready to take on the day!

Now, let's explore the power of empathy. Picture this: your best friend is struggling, and you can sense their sadness. Show them you care by lending an empathetic ear, offering a warm hug, or even a handwritten note to let them know you're there for them. By practicing empathy, you support others, strengthen your emotional intelligence, and create deeper connections.

Lastly, let's unleash the superhero within you—the power of embracing vulnerability. Society often tells us that vulnerability is a weakness, but guess what? It's a superpower! Sharing your fears, dreams, and insecurities with trusted friends or family members allows you to develop authentic relationships and discover a newfound strength within yourself. Remember, true power comes from being genuine and embracing your imperfections.

Here are three points that sum this up:

Point 1: Acknowledge and Express Your Feelings

It's crucial to recognize and honor your emotions. Remember, feeling a range of emotions is okay—it's part of being human.

Here are some tips to help you navigate your feelings:

- ❖ **Identify Your Emotions:** Take a moment to check in with yourself daily. Ask yourself how you're feeling and why. Are you happy, sad, stressed, or excited? Identifying your emotions can help you understand yourself better.

- ❖ **Find Healthy Outlets**: Expressing your feelings is vital. Creative activities like drawing, painting, or playing music can also help express emotions. Also, find supportive friends and family to talk to.

- ❖ **Seek Support:** Along with friends, having a support network that includes family members, mentors, or role models is essential. They can provide guidance, wisdom, and a shoulder to lean on during challenging times.

Point to Ponder
Why is it beneficial to acknowledge how you feel?

_____

_____

Point 2: Engage in Self-Care
Stress is no stranger to us. Everyone has moments when we feel its presence. So we must pay attention to it and get a handle on it.

Let's explore some self-care practices and stress management techniques:

❖ **Prioritize Self-Care**: Make time for activities that bring you joy and relaxation. It could be reading a book, walking in nature, practicing yoga, or indulging in a hobby. Remember, self-care is not selfish – it's necessary for your overall well-being.

❖ **Set Healthy Boundaries:** Learn to set boundaries to protect your emotional well-being. Say no when you feel overwhelmed, and don't be afraid to prioritize your needs. Healthy boundaries help maintain a healthy balance in your life.

❖ **Manage Stress:** Stress is a part of life, but how we manage it makes a difference. Try stress-reducing techniques like deep breathing exercises, listening to calming music, or engaging in physical activities like dancing or playing sports. Find what works best for you to unwind and recharge.

Point to Ponder
In what way will you commit to self-care?

_____

_____

Point 3: Develop Positive Relationships

Having positive relationships can significantly impact your emotional well-being. Here's how you can encourage healthy connections:

❖ **Seek Supportive Friends:** Seek friendships built on trust, respect, and shared interests. Healthy relationships provide a safe space to express yourself and be accepted for who you are.

❖ **Communicate Openly:** Effective communication is the foundation of healthy relationships. Express your feelings and needs honestly and encourage your friends to do the same. This expression promotes understanding and empathy and strengthens your bond.

Tips for Nurturing Your Emotional Well-Being:

❖ **Practice Gratitude:** Reflect on what you're grateful for each day. It can be as simple as a sunny day, a kind gesture, or a delicious meal. Focusing on gratitude helps shift your mindset toward positivity.

❖ **Engage in Physical Activity:** Regular exercise benefits your physical health and releases endorphins, boosting mood. Find activities you enjoy, whether dancing, hiking, or practicing a sport.

❖ **Limit Screen Time:** Excessive screen time can impact your emotional well-being. Set boundaries on social media usage and take breaks to engage in other activities that nourish your mind and body.

Remember, your emotional well-being is unique and personal to you. Make your mental health a priority. Embrace your emotions, practice self-care, develop positive relationships, and seek support when needed. Investing in your emotional well-being builds a solid foundation for a happier and healthier you.

Point to Ponder
Why should you cultivate positive relationships?

_____

_____

Affirmation
"I trust myself to make choices that align with my emotional well-being and honor my needs."

I WILL BE DRAMA FREE

Reflect and Write

1. List three ways you will set healthy boundaries for your emotional well-being.

_____

_____

_____

_____

_____

_____

_____

2. What activities will you do to protect your emotional well-being?

_____

_____

_____

_____

_____

_____

_____

_____

_____

_____

3. Why is practicing empathy towards others important?

_____

_____

_____

_____

_____

_____

_____

_____

_____

4. Why is it necessary to have a strong support network?

_____

_____

_____

_____

_____

_____

_____

_____

_____

_____

_____

Bonus for Empowering Your Emotions

Meet London, Irene, and Margo – the fearless trio who became known as the "Emotion Empowerment Squad." They believed in the power of expressing their feelings and supporting each other through thick and thin. Armed with their casual yet empowering attitudes, they set out to conquer the ups and downs of teenage life.

They faced the usual dramas and rollercoaster emotions of being a teenager. But instead of letting the chaos consume them, they acknowledged their feelings and nurtured their well-being, proving that they were more than just a bunch of high school clichés.

One sunny afternoon, London shared her recent heartbreak as they gathered at their favorite spot in the school courtyard. Her crush had chosen someone else for the upcoming dance. Instead of wallowing in sadness, her friends rallied around her. Irene suggested they host a self-love movie marathon with popcorn and face masks. They spent the evening reminding each other of their worth.

A few weeks later, Margo was overwhelmed by stress from exams and extracurricular activities. The Emotion Empowerment Squad was not having that. Instead, they organized a "Well-being Wednesday" to exchange tips and tricks for managing stress. Margo discovered meditation, London found solace in journaling, and Irene uncovered the joy of a good workout. They discovered that nurturing their well-being was necessary for maintaining their sanity amidst the chaos of high school.

As the school year progressed, they noticed a pattern. Drama seemed to follow them wherever they went. Instead of running away from it, they decided to face it head-on. They created a "Drama-Free Zone" in London's bedroom, with cozy blankets and a playlist of empowering anthems. They retreated to this safe place whenever the drama reared its ugly head, allowing themselves to vent and recharge their emotional batteries. They laughed, cried, and reminded each other that they were stronger together.

Word about the Emotion Empowerment Squad spread throughout the school, attracting other girls who were tired of being defined by drama. They organized monthly workshops where they shared their stories and discussed strategies for nurturing their well-being. These sessions became a platform for embracing vulnerability and realizing it was okay not to be okay sometimes.

By the end of the school year, the Emotion Empowerment Squad had become a recognizable force for good. Their casual language and genuine empathy drew others in and positively impacted the school. The drama didn't disappear entirely, but their approach changed. Instead of being swept away by it, they chose to empower themselves and take care of their emotional well-being.

As they tossed their graduation caps, the Emotion Empowerment Squad knew they had achieved something extraordinary. They had shown that being a teenager didn't mean being consumed by drama. They had created a supportive community where girls could empower their emotions and embrace their true selves.

And so, their legacy lived on, inspiring future generations of girls to stand tall, embrace their emotions, and nurture their well-being, no matter what dramas life threw their way.

What are your thoughts about this scenario?

_____

_____

_____

_____

_____

_____

_____

_____

_____

_____

_____

_____

_____

_____

_____

_____

_____

_____

_____

_____

_____

_____

WATCH ME BLOOM

Emotions

When emotions swirl and twist inside,
Teenage girls, don't let them hide,
It's okay to feel; it's okay to cry,
Let's ride this wave, you and I.

First, anger flares, a fiery spark. It's alright, but don't embark
On harsh actions or words that sting,
Pause, take a breath, and let patience ring.

Sadness creeps, a heavyweight, Tears may fall, don't hesitate,
Reach out to friends, let them be near,
They'll lend a shoulder and wipe each tear.

When joy bursts forth, like stars above,
Laugh out loud, embrace the love,
In moments sweet, cherish the glee,
Let happiness flow wild and free.

Anxiety's shadow, it may cast,
Don't let it hold you in its grasp,
Ground yourself in calming ways,
Find peace amidst life's hectic maze.

With envy, green, it's hard to cope,
Comparisons can steal your hope,
Remember, you're unique and bright,
Your journey shines in its own light.
Teenage girls, emotions flow. Let them come; let them go.
Through ups and downs, you'll find your way,
With casual grace, you'll seize the day.

GO AND BE THE STAR YOU ARE

A GIRL'S GUIDE TO BEING GREAT

10 TRAITS TO BE GREAT

Here are some top traits to help you have a *positive, promising,* and *productive life.*

❖ **Confidence**: Believe in yourself and your abilities. Own your unique qualities and talents. For example, strut into that interview with your head held high, knowing you've got what it takes to nail it.

❖ **Resilience:** Bounce back from setbacks and keep pushing forward. Don't allow difficulties or criticisms to break you. If you stumble, dust yourself off and stand back up. Then keep it moving!

❖ **Self-discipline**: Stay focused and committed to your goals. It means putting in the effort, even when you don't like it. So, resist the temptation to binge-watch that show when you know you have homework.

❖ **Curiosity:** Be hungry for knowledge and eager to learn. Ask questions, explore new ideas, and seek out different perspectives. Embrace the adventure of discovering the world around you, whether it's through books, documentaries, or YouTube.

❖ **Adaptability:** Embrace change and be flexible. Life throws curveballs, but you have the agility to dodge them or knock them out of the park! Whether adjusting to a new school, trying a different extracurricular activity, or moving to a new town, roll with the punches and find creative solutions.

❖ **Empathy**: Show kindness and understanding towards others. Put yourself in their shoes, listen with an open heart, and lend a helping hand. You never know the impact a small act of compassion can have on someone's day.

❖ **Time management**: Stay organized and prioritize your tasks. Balance your schoolwork, extracurricular activities, social life, and self-care. So, don't leave that project until the last minute and end up pulling an all-nighter. Instead, plan and tackle things one step at a time.

❖ **Initiative**: Take the lead and be proactive. Please don't wait for opportunities to come to you; go out and grab them! Start that club you've been dreaming of, volunteer for projects, or speak up when you have ideas worth sharing. Be the captain of your ship.

❖ **Collaboration:** Work well with others and be a team player. Whether it's group projects, sports teams, or community initiatives, bring your strengths to the table and support your teammates. Together, you can achieve more than you ever could alone.

❖ **Authenticity**: Be true to yourself and embrace your individuality. Don't be a carbon copy of someone else. Embrace your quirks, passions, and unique style. Being genuine and staying true to who you are will attract real connections and opportunities.

Apply these concepts to your life, and you will set yourself on a path to becoming a healthy and happy young lady who accomplishes remarkable things and leaves her mark on the world. On the next page, check out some girls doing just that.

TAKING ACTION FOR CHANGE

These individuals have made significant contributions and promoted positive change in their communities and beyond.

Marley Dias:

Bio: Marley Dias is an American activist and author. She launched the campaign #1000BlackGirlBooks in 2015 to collect and donate children's books that feature Black girls as the main characters. Dias has since become a prominent advocate for diversity and inclusion in literature.

Source: Time - Marley Dias (https://time.com/5171736/marley-dias-next-generation-leaders/)

Isra Hirsi:

Bio: Isra Hirsi is an American climate and racial justice activist. She co-founded the U.S. Youth Climate Strike and has actively raised awareness about climate change and its intersection with social justice issues. Hirsi has spoken at various events and is a prominent voice for youth activism.

Source: Teen Vogue - 9 Things to Know About Isra Hirsi, the Teen Climate Activist You Need to Follow (https://www.teenvogue.com/story/isra-hirsi-profile)

Brea Baker:

Bio: Brea Baker is an American activist and organizer focused on racial and social justice issues. She participated in numerous campaigns and movements and youth-led activism. Baker is a powerful advocate for marginalized communities and uses her platform to drive meaningful change.

Source: Essence - Brea Baker Wants To Make Being An Activist A Full-Time Gig (https://www.essence.com/news/breabaker-profile/)

Naomi Wadler:

Bio: Naomi Wadler is an American youth activist known for advocating against gun violence and including Black women and girls in social justice movements. At the age of 11, she gained national attention for her speech at the March for Our Lives rally in Washington, D.C., calling attention to the disproportionate impact of gun violence on Black women.

Source: CNN - Naomi Wadler: 'I wanted to represent the African American girls whose stories don't make the front page.' (https://www.cnn.com/2018/03/26/us/naomi-wadler-march-for-our-lives/index.html)

Amika George:

Bio: Amika George is a British activist and founder of the "Free Periods" campaign. She has been fighting to end period poverty in the United Kingdom and raise awareness about the issue globally. George successfully campaigned for the UK government to provide free menstrual products in schools.

Source: The Guardian - Amika George: the teenager who forced the UK government to confront period poverty (https://www.theguardian.com/lifeandstyle/2019/may/19/amika-george-the-teenager-who-forced-the-uk-government-to-confront-period-poverty)

Autumn Peltier:

Bio: Autumn Peltier is a Canadian water rights advocate and member of the Wiikwemkoong First Nation. She has been an outspoken advocate for clean water and indigenous rights. Peltier has spoken at various international forums, including the United Nations, raising awareness about the importance of water conservation and protection.
Source: CBC Kids News - 8 things to know about Autumn Peltier
(https://www.cbc.ca/kidsnews/post/8-things-to-know-about-autumn-peltier)

Mari Copeny (Little Miss Flint):

Bio: Mari Copeny, also known as Little Miss Flint, gained national attention in 2016 when she wrote a letter to then-President Barack Obama, urging him to visit Flint and address the water crisis affecting her community. At the time, Mari was just eight years old. Since then, she has continued to raise awareness about the ongoing water crisis, advocate for clean water access, and fight for children's rights in Flint and beyond.

Source: Teen Vogue - Meet the 13-Year-Old Activist Fighting for Flint's Clean Water: Mari Copeny, aka Little Miss Flint (https://www.teenvogue.com/story/mari-copeny-little-miss-flint-profile)

If you are feeling inspired, read more about these remarkable young ladies. But I encourage you to go one step further. You are a change agent, so create change that inspires others.

I Am A FUTURE Phenomenal WOMAN

A Girl's Guide to Being Great

GIRL POWER PLAYLIST

This playlist aims to uplift and empower teen girls through positive, inspiring, and clean songs. Let the music remind you of your strength, resilience, and limitless potential!

Song: "Brave"
Singer: Sara Bareilles
Bio: Sara Bareilles is an American singer-songwriter known for her powerful vocals and inspiring lyrics. "Brave" is an uplifting anthem that encourages girls to embrace their true selves, conquer their fears, and stand up for what they believe in.

Song: "Fight Song"
Singer: Rachel Platten
Bio: Rachel Platten is an American pop singer-songwriter who gained recognition with her hit single "Fight Song." The song became many's anthem of strength and determination, speaking about overcoming obstacles.

Song: "Roar"
Singer: Katy Perry
Bio: Katy Perry is an American pop icon known for her energetic performances and empowering music. "Roar" became an instant hit with its catchy melody and lyrics about finding one's voice and inner strength.

Song: "Stronger (What Doesn't Kill You)"
Singer: Kelly Clarkson
Bio: Kelly Clarkson is an American singer-songwriter who rose to fame after winning the first season of American Idol. "Stronger (What Doesn't Kill You)" is an empowering pop anthem encouraging girls to find strength in their struggles.

Song: "Girl on Fire"
Singer: Alicia Keys
Bio: Alicia Keys is an American singer-songwriter known for her soulful voice and empowering lyrics. "Girl on Fire" is a celebration of female strength and resilience.

Song: "Unstoppable"
Singer: Sia
Bio: Sia is an Australian singer-songwriter and music video director known for her powerful vocals. "Unstoppable" is a soaring anthem that encourages resilience and inner strength. The song's anthemic chorus, Sia's powerful vocal performance, and its motivational lyrics make it an empowering girl power song.

Song: "Confident"
Singer: Demi Lovato
Bio: Demi Lovato is an American singer and actress known for her powerful vocals and advocacy for mental health. "Confident" is a powerful pop anthem encouraging girls to embrace their strength, stand up for themselves, and believe in their abilities.

Song: "Scars to Your Beautiful"
Singer: Alessia Cara
Bio: Alessia Cara is a Canadian singer-songwriter. "Scars to Your Beautiful" promotes self-acceptance and challenges societal beauty standards. The song's raw honesty, Alessia's moving delivery, and message of embracing one's uniqueness make it a profoundly empowering and relatable anthem.

Song: "Unwritten"
Singer: Natasha Bedingfield
Bio: Natasha Bedingfield is a British singer known for her cheerful and inspirational songs. "Unwritten" encourages girls to embrace individuality and write their life stories.

REFERENCES

(2010). Fascinating facts about diamonds. *GIA*.
http://www.gia.edu/nav/toolbar/newsroom/articles
-for-public/article-diamonds-fascinating-facts.html.

Kent K. (2001). The paradoxical commandments. New York:
G. P. Putnam's Sons.

A Girl's Guide to Being Great

Congratulations!

You have just completed "A Girl's Guide to Being Great." You are now in the company of thousands of girls! You, like them, have the knowledge and tools to help you become a "great girl" and a great woman.
The power is in your hands.

If this book benefited you, reach out to me. Please share your thoughts about the book, what you learned, or how you're becoming a "great girl." Email me at:

Rhonda@rhondamincey.com.

I am cheering you on!

Ms. Rhonda Mincey

A GIRL'S GUIDE TO BEING GREAT